Finding Mercy on the Way of Sorrow

40 DAILY REFLECTIONS
FROM THE **BOOK OF LAMENTATIONS**

Finding Mercy on the Way of Sorrow

AN EASTER DEVOTIONAL

ROBIN HAM

10 Publishing
a division of **10** of**those**.com

Copyright © 2024 by Robin Ham

First published in Great Britain in 2024

Parts of this devotional on Lamentations were previously published as daily Bible reading notes in Explore by The Good Book Company, 2020, and are used by kind permission.

British Library Cataloguing in Publication Data
A record for this book is available from the British Library

ISBN: 978-1-915705-52-5

Designed by Pete Barnsley (CreativeHoot.com)

Printed in Denmark

10Publishing, a division of 10ofthose.com
Unit C, Tomlinson Road, Leyland, PR25 2DY, England

Email: info@10ofthose.com
Website: www.10ofthose.com

1 3 5 7 10 8 6 4 2

For Mum & Dad – thank you for everything.
Lam. 5:19

Contents

Acknowledgments

Scripture is always best read together with others. I'm grateful to Carl Laferton, who first gave me the opportunity to write on Lamentations for the Good Book Company's Explore series back in 2020. A few years later, it was my friend Tom who suggested Lamentations would be the perfect book to journey through in Lent. I have to say that suggestion has raised a few eyebrows since then – but my own experience has been to deeply appreciate Lamentations' fresh invitation to a life of honest faith and heartfelt repentance. I've been especially helped by the sage and sincere reflections on this tender portion of Scripture from (amongst others) Adele Berlin, Dave Bish, Paul House, Alianore Smith, Colin Smith, Andrew Towner, Mark Vroegop, Barry Webb, C.J. Williams and Christopher Wright. A special acknowledgment feels apt for Tim Keller, whose writing and speaking on and through suffering, even as he approached his own death, is a legacy in itself.

I've realised that behind every published piece of writing is a diligent but often unseen team, so I'd like to acknowledge Lois at 10ofThose and my editor Julie, who were both hugely patient and considerate as these forty devotions came together!

I'm also grateful to my sisters and brothers at St Paul's Church, Barrow, who showed me understanding as I worked on this devotional, and amongst whom are countless precious examples of walking the 'way of sorrow', which it is a privilege to learn from.

Lastly, my heart is full of thanks to God for my wife, Zoe, and our kids, who have not rolled their eyes too much when I've said (frequently!) over the past eighteen months, 'Well, it's not *quite* finished.' But more than just being grateful for them waiting for me, ultimately I rejoice that I get to do life amidst their hope-filled rhythms of waiting for someone much greater!

Let us say together, 'The Lord is our portion; therefore we will wait for him.'

Introduction to Lamentations

'Life is pain, your highness. Anyone who says differently is selling something.'

Those honest words are spoken by the mysterious character Dread Pirate Roberts to Princess Buttercup in William Goldman's hilarious cult film (and book!), *The Princess Bride*. (If you've not seen it, please borrow my copy!)

In the scene, Buttercup is taken aback by the bluntness of the words, but when you give them a few seconds of thought, they are refreshing words too. Suffering is *inescapable*. It's as certain as, well, death and taxes (although I guess they're hardly unrelated!). We're all sinners in a suffering world and we're all sufferers in a sinful world. Anyone – or, we might add, any philosophy, religion or *even* portrayal of Christianity – that says differently is probably 'selling something', or at least is guilty of misrepresenting the reality of life.

And that's why we need Lamentations.

THREE FACTORS WHY LAMENTATIONS IS UNFAMILIAR GROUND

In my experience, Lamentations is not a section of the Bible that many Christians know especially well. A few years ago, there was a viral online quiz going round where you had to work out whether each quote was a verse from Lamentations or a Taylor Swift lyric. Admittedly, the Bible verses were from *The Message* paraphrase, but

I think the fact that so many people struggled shows it's hardly a book in which the Western church has been immersed. (It's either that or Taylor's less popular than she used to be!)

But, to be fair, there are probably a few factors explaining Lamentations' unfamiliarity to us.

1. Lamentations is poetry

Instinctively many of us are drawn to the logic or application of New Testament epistles, or to our beloved Old Testament narratives, or even to the familiarity of the Gospels. But poetry often feels like a 'gear change'. Ever tried to *analyse* a poem? As any good English teacher will say, such detailed study is not really the point. Perhaps we steer clear because, tragically, the church hasn't been great at demonstrating the value of the poetic books of the Bible.

2. Lamentations connects us to an unfamiliar moment in Bible history

We find ourselves in the sixth century BC, when the city of Jerusalem has been laid to waste by a neighbouring nation, the Babylonians. It's hardly an obvious place to preach from, especially if all we want is 'Seven Steps to a Successful Year with Jesus'. How do we relate to this? Maybe we think we or others will struggle to connect, and so we park Lamentations to one side – and stick to something that seems more obvious.

3. Lamentations is just grim

There's no two ways about it. Lamentations is heavy and sombre and unrelenting. Don't people need something a bit more upbeat? A bit easier on the ear? After all, no one likes to end up sitting next to the moaner at the party. Isn't it the same with Lamentations?

But what if this neglect of Lamentations was all to our detriment? What if we were missing out on something that was actually good for our spiritual health? And not just missing out individually, but missing out as the twenty-first-century Western church at large?

THREE REASONS WHY LAMENTATIONS IS A PRECIOUS PLACE TO DWELL THIS LENT

So let me give you three reasons to stick with Lamentations this Lent…

1. Lamentations is a vital spiritual resource to help us honestly process suffering

With Lamentations, the clue is in the name! But how often does the language of lament feature in our churches? My sense is not so much, which is probably a bit odd if suffering is unavoidable. More than that, if we perpetuate a form of Christianity that is uncomfortable with talking about suffering, we will end up with churches where people either feel they've got to hide their pain or where hurting people simply limp away.

Lamentations is a healthy corrective. It gives us words for confession, exasperation, doubt, shame, longing, pain and injustice. Even the style of the writing evokes sorrow. To use the technical words, its rhythmic metre is a dirge. Even if you heard the original Hebrew and knew nothing of what it meant, you'd still pick up the sadness in the style.

For this reason, and perhaps in contrast to contemporary Christianity, Lamentations has been a much-prized book throughout Jewish history. Every year on the ninth day of the Hebrew month, *Av*, it is read aloud, allowing people to remember Jerusalem's destruction in 587 BC, but also to acknowledge, process and respond to all suffering. One writer, Leslie C. Allen, called his book on Lamentations *Liturgy of Grief*.[1] Or, as Mark Vroegop puts it, Lamentations 'shows us how to pray when the dark clouds of suffering roll in.'[2]

2. Lamentations brings us up close and personal with the seriousness of human sin

As we get our bearings in Lamentations, we'll discover the book does not hold back about all that is wrong with the world. Lamentations gives us a wide-angle view on the impact of human rebellion and the reality of sin. This brings with it both razor-sharp, personal challenge, but also huge, explanatory power. Initially, Lamentations might seem to describe a foreign landscape, and yet as we look closer, we'll see a landscape we recognise. We may not be living in Jerusalem in 587 BC, but we're all living amidst the devastating effects of sin and with the shadows of God's coming judgment cast over us.

Yes, there will be *particular* aspects to the sin and suffering in Lamentations that we'll need to consider carefully. We'll need to think about how we apply this portion of God's word to ourselves as those living in between Jesus' first and second appearings. We'll also need to think about what difference it makes to read Lamentations as Christians who have been forgiven. But there's no getting round the way Lamentations will hold up a mirror to our hearts and show us sin is a big deal.

3. Lamentations teaches a suffering church how to find authentic hope

The most famous verses in Lamentations are right at the physical centre of the book:

> *Because of the LORD's great love we are not consumed,*
> *   for his compassions never fail.*
> *They are new every morning;*
> *   great is your faithfulness.*
> (3:22–23)

Maybe you recognise them, or can see the way those verses have inspired hymns and worship songs?

They are wonderful verses, but they're so much more than just cheery soundbites that look good on an Instagram picture. These come right in the middle of five profoundly moving poems of lament.

In fact, though it's not obvious in our English translations, chapters one to four all follow an ordered 'acrostic' pattern in the original Hebrew. This means the first line of each poem begins with the first letter of the Hebrew alphabet, the second line begins with the second letter, and so on – all the way from the Hebrew equivalent of 'A' to 'Z'.

Why does that matter? Because in the chaos of suffering, grief and loss, God does not shut us down with trite one-liners. Instead he walks with us along a tenderly-crafted path that helps us process the depths of our sorrow.

As we hike through Lamentations' dark valleys, rather than offering us merely 'feel-good Christianity' or a triumphalist faith that seems disconnected with real life, we instead discover something richer, sweeter and more substantial: the covenant mercy of God.

THE AUTHOR OF LAMENTATIONS

Historically, it's been common to assume the writer was the prophet Jeremiah. He certainly lived at the same time as the destruction of Jerusalem. For lots of other reasons, that analysis makes sense. But there are also some good reasons why it may not have been Jeremiah.

To be honest, nothing hangs on the author's identity. Whoever he was, he's bared his soul with five heart-wrenching laments, and yet they're also spectacularly crafted, as we'll hopefully see. For that reason, we'll just call him 'the poet'!

Approaching the Season of Lent

WHAT'S THE DEAL WITH LENT?

For some of you, even the idea of a season of 'Lent' might not be particularly familiar. You certainly won't find the word 'lent' in the Bible – so marking Lent can't be obligatory for Christians! Rather, I'd place Lent in the category of 'human traditions that God might choose to graciously use for our growth'! For example, we know that from as early as the fourth century, Christians had crafted a special annual calendar to journey through the key events in the life of Jesus. And just like Christmas and Easter, Lent was part of that calendar, setting aside forty days in the run up to Jesus' death and resurrection.

Historically, the emphasis at Lent has been on developing a rhythm of confessing our sin, confronting our mortality and hungering for God's salvation in Jesus Christ. Every Lent is a reminder that we need a Saviour. The actual word simply comes from 'lengthen', a reference to the hours of daylight getting longer again in springtime. As life prepares to burst out of the natural world around us, so we prepare our hearts for the good news of Jesus' death and resurrection. By the way, the forty days (excluding Sundays) of Lent picks up on the rich biblical associations with that number: forty days of waiting for the flood to end in Genesis; forty years wandering in the wilderness for the nation of Israel; forty days that Jesus was tempted in the desert.

As for my choice of Lamentations in Lent, I was encouraged to discover there's a long tradition of Christians dwelling in Lamentations during Lent. Going back as far as the eighth century, it would be read and sung particularly during Holy Week. But actually that shouldn't be a surprise! With its focus on humility, contrition and dependence, Lamentations is the perfect soundtrack to Lent.

USING THIS DEVOTIONAL

If you journeyed through the book of Ruth in my Advent devotional, *Finding Hope Under Bethlehem Skies*, then you'll recognise the format here. There are forty daily, written reflections, one for every day in Lent – you can have a breather with your church family on Sundays!

For each day, you'll be encouraged to read a few verses from Lamentations and then a written reflection. Next are little suggestions or questions for further consideration and prayer. You might like to commit to reading the reflections with a friend or discipleship group and then discussing these closing questions together.

Each day's reflection then ends with a suggested song or version of a hymn by way of a response. These can easily be found online, but we've compiled a Spotify playlist that includes them all – just search for 'Finding Mercy' on the Spotify app.

Whether or not you've come across Lent before, I pray that by God's Spirit we all may come more fully alive to the depth of our need, but also to the overwhelming provision of God's grace in Jesus Christ.

Loving Father,
In this season of lengthening days,
increase our awareness of your mercy.
How wide and deep and long it is!

You call us to turn from the long shadows
of our sin and lean upon Jesus Christ.
Guard me from denying my brokenness and mortality,
and astonish me afresh that I am beloved.
By your Spirit, fill me with a hunger for you, more than anything in
this world.
Rather than beating ourselves up, instead lift Christ up in our hearts.
Help us to 'survey the wondrous cross' from new angles, and to grasp
your grace in new ways this Lent.
In Jesus' name, Amen.

Day 1: Ash Wednesday

A Day of Ash in the City of Ashes

Read Lamentations 1:1a

WELCOME TO THE CITY

Take a good look around you, but first, be warned: it's not a pretty sight. Here lies the remains of a city, and not just any old 'big smoke'. This one was special – we call it '*the* city' (1:1; my italics).

Once 'the city' was so full of people, but now it's deserted. Once a picture of life, now it's deathly quiet. Once a people and a place that told the world a story of grace, now these smouldering ruins tell another story – of anguish, guilt and despair.

Is Google Maps not working for you? Let me help you: this is *Jerusalem* – and it's 587 BC. *Welcome*, if that's the right word. And welcome to Lamentations. All around is rubble and ash. And that smell? That's hopelessness. In these parts, it lingers thick in the air.

Maybe you're starting to wonder why you've come? But let me tell you, there are few better places to be on Ash Wednesday.

BROUGHT BACK DOWN TO EARTH

For hundreds of years of Christian tradition, Ash Wednesday marked the beginning of the season of Lent. Think of it as a day to bring us back down to earth. After all, we are all on a collision course to be reunited with the earth from which we came: 'for dust you are and to dust you will return' (Genesis 3:19).

It is not simply that death is inevitable. Lent isn't about 'looking death in the eye', 'seizing the day' and making fresh 'bucket lists'.

Instead, Lent involves acknowledging that death is our inevitable sentence because a verdict has been justly passed. The apostle Paul puts it clearly enough: 'the wages of sin is death' (Romans 6:23).

For some of us, death will feel close right now. Too close, probably. Maybe it's the debilitation of illness. Maybe it's the persistent ache of grief. Maybe it's that sense of life unravelling before our eyes; age and circumstance and loss...

And for those waking up in Jerusalem in 587 BC, death was also unavoidable. *Every* day was Ash Wednesday.

HOW...?!

Take a look again at the opening word of Lamentations in 1:1. The Hebrew word is êkâ, which perhaps best translates as 'How?!' In fact, the same word also begins chapters 2 and 4 of Lamentations. But this isn't a polite question expressing puzzlement or ignorance. It's an exclamation of grief and sorrow: *How ... can this be?! How ... on earth?! How ... long must this last?! How ... the mighty have fallen?!*

You're probably getting a sense of Lamentations' tone already. Well, we ain't seen nothing yet. But stick with it. Yes, we begin Lent by confronting our mortality, but the surprisingly liberating truth wired into the rhythm of Ash Wednesday is that the way down is the way up. We die to find life. We walk towards the grave, but the tomb is empty.

So whether or not you're familiar with Lent, and whether or not you've spent much time in Lamentations, I pray that this journey might take us to places of surprising hope.

Almighty and Everlasting God, who hates nothing that you have made and who forgives the sins of all who turn to you: over these coming weeks, create and shape in us humble hearts, that as we face up to our brokenness and sin, we may receive from you, the God of all mercy, the Spirit-filled gift of repentance, fresh assurance of forgiveness and lavish helpings of hope – through Jesus Christ our Lord. Amen. (Adapted from the Book of Common Prayer)

 Listen to '*Ash Wednesday's Early Morn*' by Liturgical Folk and Lauren Plank Goans.

The A to Z of Suffering

Read Lamentations 1:1–3

THE LONELY WOMAN

With Lamentations, the clue is in the name. And yet 'lament' isn't particularly common today – at least not within a formal Christian setting. Can you recall hearing someone preach on a psalm of lament? Have you witnessed public prayers deeply acknowledging the pain that people in your church were facing? When did your discipleship group last cry out to God about the state of the world?

Lamentations will help us receive God's gift of lament. But in order to do that, we're going to meet a person.

Yesterday we were shown around a city, but now this city is portrayed as a woman – a widow in grief (1:1). And her story is one of a dramatic reversal: she was a queen, but has become a slave. We hear her sobs of anguish in the night, all alone, with no one to comfort her (1:2). Are you ready for this?

LONG TIME COMING

So what's going on? God's people had been on a downward spiral ever since splitting into two kingdoms. Verse 3 refers to the nation of Judah, which was the southern and remaining kingdom of God's people. The northern kingdom, often known simply as Israel, had been invaded and decimated by the Assyrian army nearly two hundred years before. It had been a punishment for her idolatry, and Judah in the south was meant to heed the warning.

But now her time was up too. As we see hinted at, she had been unfaithful to God: 'among all her lovers there is no one to comfort her' (1:2). Lovers, plural? Jerusalem is not simply a widow facing bereavement, she is an unfaithful partner whose infidelity has left her alone. And now those 'who pursue her have overtaken her' (1:3) – this time, as the book of 2 Kings tells us, the conquerors were the Babylonian empire. It all culminated in a final siege of Judah's capital, Jerusalem, before she too fell in 586 BC. Lamentations is born out of *that* experience.

EAVESDROPPING ON GRIEF

We all know how deeply personal grief is. When we see someone tearing up or sobbing uncontrollably, part of us might want to instinctively step back and give them some space. Or maybe we just turn away, feeling uncomfortable at their vulnerability.

And yet often we can't help being drawn to watch and listen too. The emotion is real and visceral in a world that is often superficial.

Here, in Lamentations, God wants us to step closer. To lean in to these laments and feel their heart. And because they are written in this ordered 'acrostic' form, the unwieldy nature of suffering can now be expressed in a satisfactory way. This is the A to Z of suffering.

I wonder how you're feeling about the next thirty-nine days? Lamentations is not an easy book to read, both in terms of the gut-wrenching subject matter and how we apply it to ourselves today. Spend some time praying that as Lamentations gives us this humbling vantage point on Jerusalem's suffering, we'd listen well to this grief, and that it might give us a fresh perspective on God, his world, and ourselves.

 Listen to *'Dust We Are and Shall Return'* by The Brilliance.

A Wake of Desolation

Read Lamentations 1:4–6

FAMILIAR SCENES?

In late February 2022, the media began to show devastating images from the horrific Russian invasion of Ukraine. Decimated roads. Towns battered and bruised. A wake of desolation. Yet opening our Bibles today, we see something eerily familiar. And for the first time *this* city is named: Zion (1:4, 6).

SURELY NOT THE HOLY CITY?

Originally Zion just described a specific hill in the region. Yet since King David's reign, the name became associated with the whole city of Jerusalem, and sometimes with Israel as a nation too. But it was more than a *geographical* label. It captured a sense of this place being the 'home' of God's promises. It spoke of the care that God had for this people, his 'treasured possession', tenderly personifying the city with the phrase 'Daughter Zion' (1:6). This was God's 'special one', a holy city, the dwelling place of the Lord himself.

And so to walk the road to Zion would have been a journey filled with anticipation and joy and longing. In fact, many of the Bible's psalms are songs of 'ascent' – sung by pilgrims to celebrate nearing Jerusalem. They were coming to worship God. They were coming home.

GOD IS NOT ABSENT

But now everything had changed. The only activity on these roads is mourning. Any life is in its death throes. And this left a bitter taste with the people (1:4), not simply because of the suffering they faced, but because of the loss this suffering revealed.

As we read on, we discover more of what has occurred in Jerusalem. Her enemies have taken hold of her – and without any real fight (1:5). Rather than being a city of blessing for her people, it is now Jerusalem's enemies who are prospering. Her young women grieve; her priests groan (1:4). Her children have been taken (1:5).

And whilst Jerusalem's unfaithfulness was hinted at yesterday, this reality now drops like a nuclear bomb: 'The LORD has brought her grief because of her many sins' (1:5).

THE EXPLANATION

The reason is both simple and stark; both unashamedly blunt *and* unrelentingly painful. Suddenly this tale of woe isn't just about the people of Jerusalem suffering at the hands of oppressors. We are introduced to a new character: the Lord himself, who has brought upon 'Daughter Zion' a due punishment for 'her many sins' (1:5). God is not absent, but rather present in a terrifying way.

This clear grasp of why Jerusalem is suffering will run throughout Lamentations. The poet never hides away from it. And it's hugely important for understanding this book as Christians. The people of Jerusalem in 587–86 BC were being punished for turning away from God. Their suffering was directly related to their sin. The word used in 1:5 speaks of a wilful breaking of God's covenant and will occur twice more in this chapter (1:14, 22). These weren't sporadic, occasional or accidental breaches.

We need to take care as we draw parallels between the situation described in Lamentations and our lives today. As we've just seen, Jerusalem's suffering was a direct consequence of her turning away from God. But that same tight causal connection is not made between all suffering and sin in our world today. For Christians, those who are now trusting in Jesus, we can be sure our suffering isn't 'condemnation', for Jesus has already taken this upon himself (Romans 8:1). And yet our poet wants to show us how to think and feel about sin and judgment. Pray the Spirit would be at work in our hearts.

 Listen to *'Brokenness Aside'* by All Sons & Daughters, featuring Leslie Jordan and David Leonard.

Day 4

Stop. Look. Listen

Read Lamentations 1:7–11

IF LOOKS COULD...

We often say, 'If looks could kill...' but actually looks can do many things. A lover catching their partner's eye over dinner. A parent's smile to their child across a crowded school hall. The cold shake of an employer's head that signals knowing disapproval. In today's passage, the running theme is of 'looks' and being seen, but in all the wrong ways. If you're reading with younger readers, be aware too that some of the language is fairly explicit.

Our poet continues to describe Jerusalem as more than a lonely widow. She has lost all her treasures and privilege, and is now being mocked and derided (1:7). In fact, these verses quickly become deeply uncomfortable: Jerusalem is 'naked' and exposed; she can't even bear to look down at herself (1:8). What is happening?

NOWHERE TO LOOK

In the surrounding cultures, the imagery here would have been associated with a woman caught in adultery. The frequent punishment of public shaming – perhaps even lifting up her skirt – would underline the horror of her unfaithfulness. This certainly fits the poet's verdict: 'Jerusalem has sinned greatly and so has become unclean' (1:8). Whatever we think of the cultural practice, it is clear that this woman has been *unfaithful*.

As if that wasn't enough, the poet then picks up again the language of her 'treasures' (1:10), but this time it is in a darker light. Groping hands are being laid upon Jerusalem; multiple people are entering her 'sanctuary', her sacred place. Sadly, the sexual allusions are clear once more. Yet where once Jerusalem had engaged wilfully with her 'lovers' (1:2), now her will is being brutally resisted.

LOOK AT ME

Amongst this horrendous imagery, we now hear the city herself speak for the first time. Twice she pleads with the God of promise, the Lord, to 'look' upon her (1:9, 11). And yet the only eyes upon Jerusalem are the unwanted gloating and disdainful stares of her enemies. They look but laugh, despising her.

How do you feel about this woman? Yes, she is evidently being held to account for her unfaithfulness. Yes, she 'did not consider her future', acting as if her actions had no consequences (1:9). Yes, she had chosen to take on forbidden lovers. But this account is written in such a way, that we cannot but pity her. It feels wrong to even be witnessing these moments. Surely anyone walking by would intervene?

It's notable that when she pleads to God, Jerusalem doesn't say 'my enemy has triumphed', but '*the* enemy …' It's as if she's raising her eyebrows to God. Is her suffering not a damning indictment on *his* reputation too? Is *his* own honour not at stake? As her original covenant partner, is her shame not his shame? And so the poet makes a point of expressing his pain directly to God. This is a powerful reminder that in lament we can approach God and urge him to act in line with his sure character.

Jerusalem pleads with God to look and see, and yet – for now – there is silence. It's a frank reminder that unfaithfulness to God has consequences. How foolish to think otherwise – to not consider our future. How do you feel reading these emotive descriptions of Jerusalem? Do they impact how you think and feel about your own sin?

And yet for the Christian, sin and shame do not have the last word. One day God himself would come down to earth to suffer nakedness, bearing our shame and facing scoffing, rejection and grief.

 Listen to *'Eve's Lament (Genesis)'* by Caroline Cobb.

Day 5

Is It Nothing to You?

Read Lamentations 1:12–13

LOOKING UPON SUFFERING

How do you respond to suffering? Imagine a friend shares news of a sudden diagnosis. Or maybe a colleague opens up about some long-running conflict in their personal life.

What about if the person suffering is not someone you particularly know? Maybe you see someone weeping on their own in a cafe. Perhaps you watch a documentary about some tragedy or injustice, with a distressing interview from a survivor.

We all recognise that to 'pass by' suffering without a response seems cold and inhumane. And yet it's easier than we think. We live in a broken world. Our newsfeeds and TV channels are full of suffering.

IS ANY SUFFERING LIKE THIS?

In today's reading, there is a change: our poet takes a step back from his narrator's perspective, and instead we hear continuously the voice of the city, still personified as a woman. This powerfully helps us experience Jerusalem's suffering first-hand.

This afflicted woman begins by asking how we will respond to her suffering (1:12). Is it nothing to us? Is there any suffering like Jerusalem's suffering?

Again, it's important we see that Lamentations is dealing with a particular kind of suffering – the unique suffering that occurs from being on the wrong side of God's righteous judgment against sin (1:12–15). This is not the same as the various sufferings we might face throughout our lives, as bitter and painful as they may be.

PASSING BY THE CROSS

Fascinatingly, when the Gospel writer Matthew records his account of Jesus' crucifixion, he chooses to describe those who make their way past the cross in strikingly similar terms to Lamentations 1:12:

> *Two rebels were crucified with him, one on his right and one on his left. Those who passed by hurled insults at him, shaking their heads and saying, 'You who are going to destroy the temple and build it in three days, save yourself! Come down from the cross, if you are the Son of God!' (Matthew 27:38–40).*

Matthew seems to want us to make a connection between Jerusalem in 587 BC and Jesus. As Jesus of Nazareth hung on a Roman cross, this was much more like Jerusalem's suffering in Lamentations than it was like any suffering that we might face in our lives. This is because the day of Jesus' death was also a day of the Lord's 'fierce anger' (Lamentations 1:12). As such, it calls for a response.

ALL YOU WHO PASS BY

Through the lens of the cross of Jesus, the powerful and painful question of Lamentations 1:12 has inspired many Christian poets and songwriters. What will our response be to Christ's suffering? The hymn-writer Charles Wesley made a connection to Lamentations in this hymn:

All ye that pass by,
To Jesus draw nigh:
To you is it nothing that Jesus should die?
Your ransom and peace,
Your surety He is;
Come, see if there ever was sorrow like His.[3]

Both Jerusalem's suffering and Jesus' suffering show us that rebellion against God is a bigger deal than we imagined. As we see these momentous events on the landscape of history, we're to conclude that God is holy and that sin has a cost. But Jesus' suffering shows us something else too: God's love for you is such that Jesus was willing to suffer a suffering like no other. Don't 'pass by' the cross today. Echo Fanny Crosby's prayer: 'Jesus, keep me near the cross'.

 Listen to *'All Ye That Pass By, to Jesus Draw Nigh'* by Lor.

Day 6

No Comfort

Read Lamentations 1:14–17

ALONE

Someone once said, 'Whilst sin's pleasures are often shared, its consequences are faced alone.' This is graphically demonstrated in Lamentations 1.

We know from the other biblical accounts of these events that Jerusalem faced a grim siege warfare (2 Kings 25). As often happened, eventually the captured prisoners would be led away, hands tied and yoked around their neck to the prisoner in front (1:14). When the last remaining soldiers of the defending army were no more, the people would be crushed and trampled upon as the city was breached (1:15).

But in today's reading, we pick up a familiar thread. Who is behind this attack? The repeated use of 'he' and 'his' leads us unflinchingly to 'the Lord' (1:15). Yes, there has been an 'army' against Jerusalem; yes, they have faced 'the hands of those [they] cannot withstand' (1:14). But it is clearly *God* who has orchestrated this onslaught.

In fact, a shocking irony is lost in our English translations of 1:15a. The original Hebrew emphasises that it is God who is in Jerusalem's midst, evoking Jerusalem's beloved refrain of Psalm 46:5: 'God is within her, she will not fall.' And yet now the desperate reality is that whilst God *is* present, it is to judge his people. He has overthrown Jerusalem's defences and rejected her warriors.

ACHING FOR THE COMFORTER

Maybe you've noticed how the phrase 'no one ... to comfort' Jerusalem (see, for example, 1:16–17) is repeated throughout this chapter. The poet began by empathetically describing this reality (1:2) and the phrase also occurs elsewhere (1:9, 21). God's people are left with 'no one to comfort' them, not because God has been overpowered or found wanting, but because they have rejected the One whose covenant comfort and blessing they enjoyed for centuries. As such, he has turned his hand against them.

But here in 1:16, the Hebrew wording is phrased slightly differently, as is better captured by these other translations:

> *For these things I weep; my eyes flow with tears; for a comforter is far from me, one to revive my spirit... (ESV).*

> *For these things I weep; mine eye, mine eye runneth down with water, because the comforter that should relieve my soul is far from me... (KJV).*

The poet tells us Jerusalem is not just missing comfort for her grief, but aches with the absence of 'the comforter' himself.

WHY I WEEP

This leads to the woman's devastating and revealing testimony of 1:16: '*This* is why I weep and my eyes overflow with tears' (my italics). Her own tears are not just tears of pain and sadness at the devastation she has faced. She weeps because she knows what she has done. She weeps because she knows she has been unfaithful. She has lost the Lord, her Comforter.

And how we should weep when we feel the sting of our sin. How we should weep when we see the ways we spurn our Creator. How we should weep after we've trampled upon the saving work of Jesus Christ, as if his death had not bought us at great price.

> *God's judgment is indeed something people face alone, with 'no one to comfort', but as we walk towards Easter, we know that Jesus faced that judgment alone for us, so that we might never be alone. As such, it's no small thing that Jesus also described the Holy Spirit as 'the Comforter'. So however dark our experience of life in this world is, we are never left to ourselves. Those in Christ can confidently hold onto his promise that the Comforter 'lives with you and will be in you' (John 14:17).*
>
> Listen to *'Oh Hope'* by Joshua Luke Smith.

Day 7

The Death of Denial

Read Lamentations 1:18–22

VINDICATING THE OSTRICH?

I once met someone who said their lifelong mission was vindicating the ostrich. They were referring to the common English idiom of telling someone in denial that they're 'being an ostrich'. As this man explained to me, ostriches aren't cowards who foolishly think they can hide themselves by sticking their head below deck. Instead, what they're actually doing is rotating their eggs to make sure they're evenly warmed in the ground. After all, being a flightless bird, building a nest in a tree isn't really an option!

But what about humans? We aren't worthy of such vindication because the human capacity for 'burying our heads in the sand' is boundless. Humans are masters of self-deception and denial. In fact, the author Keith Kahn-Harris has said we live in a 'new age of denialism'.[4]

That makes 1:18 all the more remarkable. It would have been so easy for God's people to deny their sin. To make excuses. To accuse God of being unjust. Or to blame their enemies. But what do they do instead? They confess. God is in the right; they are in the wrong.

GOD IN THE RIGHT

God's 'command' (1:18) refers to God's covenant law, given to God's people at Mount Sinai. In turning their backs on that word, the people of Jerusalem knew they had been 'most rebellious' (1:20).

The English poet John Donne captured this in a simple couplet: 'But yet the Lord is just, and righteous still; I have rebelled against his holy will.'[5] God's people are facing more than they can bear, but they understand this is not more than they deserve.

PRAYING FOR JUSTICE

We'll explore God's covenant with his people later, but as we come to the end of Lamentations 1, there is a fascinating change in emphasis. Rather than simply looking down at her own suffering and sin, Lady Jerusalem now points towards those who have mistreated her. She has just confessed that she is worthy of her punishment, but she also knows that her enemies have been rejoicing in her downfall – and so she pleads with God to judge their wickedness too (1:21–22).

These words reveal something profound about being God's covenant people. Such is the depth of love God has for his people, that even as they stagger under the weight of his judgment, they can be sure that God will punish their enemies. After all, the Babylonians were not passive in the bloodshed that had occurred on the streets of Jerusalem. Likewise, the other neighbouring nations who had watched this onslaught and rejoiced would also be held to account.

> The writer G.K. Chesterton famously called sin 'the one Christian doctrine that does not need proving'.[6] And yet it's staggering how easily we can come up with reasons or theories to excuse or explain our thoughts, words and actions. There is a refreshing honesty to the confession in 1:18. Of course, we will all be sinned against (as in 1:22), but if we've first recognised our own sin, then our cries for righteousness and justice are seared with contrition and humility. If you are very aware of being sinned against today, how does this passage encourage and challenge you?
>
> ---
>
> Listen to 'This Is Not Who I Want to Be' by Joanna Sternberg.

Day 8

A Tale of Two Cities

Read Revelation 21:1–27

THE CITY THAT WAS

If you visit the old city of Jerusalem today, you'll see the Western Wall (or so-called 'Wailing Wall'). Standing nineteen metres above ground, this line of ancient stones is where Jewish people come to mourn and pray, especially on Tisha B'Av, an annual fast day. Sometimes reading the book of Lamentations aloud, the mourners will lament various calamities in Jewish history, including the destruction of the original temple in 586 BC.

Having come to the end of Lamentations 1, we'll now begin a rhythm of reflecting after each chapter in the light of the New Testament. Today, we step back and reflect on the poet's painful personification of the city of Jerusalem, 'Daughter Zion'. Her sorrow has felt unrelenting – and yet we have been invited to share in her grief. And like those mourners in Jerusalem today, our sorrow is not just for the destruction of a physical place…

A NEW JERUSALEM

As we trace the theme of Jerusalem throughout the Bible, ultimately we are led to the apostle John's vision in Revelation. God pulls back the curtains and shows John the spiritual realities happening behind our world, culminating with the fulfilment of Isaiah's cosmic promise of 'a new heaven and a new earth' (Revelation 21:1; cf. Isaiah 65:17). And right in the centre of this new creation is *another* city: 'I saw the Holy City, the new Jerusalem, coming down out of heaven from God, prepared as a bride beautifully dressed for her husband' (Revelation 21:2).

The significance of this 'new' city is that it embodies 'God's dwelling-place … now [being] among the people' (21:3). God's realm, heaven, is reunited with our realm, earth. It is like Eden but better, because sin has been dealt with – and so God wipes every tear from his people's eyes (21:4).

A CITY OR A PEOPLE?

But just as Lamentations 1 describes a person that is really a city, John is shown a city that could also be a person – or persons! Throughout the Scriptures, bridal imagery is distinctly used for the people of God (see, for example, Isaiah 61:10; Matthew 9:15; Ephesians 5:22–33; 2 Corinthians 11:2). This city is not just 'like' a bride (Revelation 21:2); she *is* 'the bride, the wife of the Lamb' (21:9), the church.

What's going on? Bible scholars point out that apocalyptic literature (such as the book of Revelation) is known for often 'mixing its metaphors'. We're meant to 'look twice'! This new Jerusalem is probably intentionally both a city and a people. For God to be with his people, we need a *place*. But for that place to mean anything, it is filled with a *people*.

And the imagery shows that ultimately what is crucial is the city's relationship with the Bridegroom, 'the Lamb', Jesus Christ. When he walked this earth, Jesus declared his own body to be the new temple (John 2:19; Mark 14:58), for he was the ultimate dwelling place between God and sinful people (John 1:14). As such, this city needs no 'temple', for *he* is there (Revelation 21:22).

Do you ache for this city to come? Sometimes Christians can be guilty of presenting the Christian hope for the future in a glib manner that ignores, or rushes past, the realities of sin and death that still ravage our world. But Lamentations is a gift because it 'tunes our hearts' to ache – for a place where God will come to dwell with his people.

We should feel this 'holy discontent' as we live in a broken world awaiting the fullness of God's promise. Just as 'Daughter Zion' groans, so the Spirit teaches us to groan for what is to come (Romans 8:18–27). That is why John's final words in response to this 'new Jerusalem' are a heartfelt longing for Jesus to return: 'Come, Lord Jesus' (Revelation 22:20).

 Listen to *'All Things New'* by Hymn Collective and Red Mountain Church.

Day 9

God in the Spotlight

Read Lamentations 2:1–4

SEEING GOD CLEARLY

'What comes into our minds when we think about God is the most important thing about us.' So said the Christian writer A.W. Tozer. In other words, few things in life will have as much impact upon us as our understanding of what God is like. And Lamentations 2 is going to challenge us to consider whether our personal perspective on God quite fits the reality.

We're in a new lament, but our poet again carefully crafts his words. He uses the same methodical acrostic structure as before with the first line starting with a word beginning with 'A', the next with 'B', the next with 'C' and so on, bringing a sense of order amidst the disorientating carnage. And we begin with the same opening exclamation of shock as chapter 1: 'How…?!' (2:1).

But then things become a little different. Whereas the first chapter focused primarily on 'she', Jerusalem, powerfully personifying the city as a sorrowful woman, this second chapter focuses repeatedly on a different character: 'He… He… He…' (2:1–4). With sombre intensity, the spotlight falls almost exclusively on *God*.

And if chapter 1 was shocking, chapter 2 should probably come with a warning: 'Some viewers may find these scenes upsetting.' But though it may at times feel uncomfortable, we can't avoid their inclusion in Holy Scripture. Will we see God for who he is?

GOD'S HOLINESS IN ACTION

Often our talk about God's attributes and character can seem abstract and theoretical. Not so here. God displays his character in his actions. Yes, these are poetical descriptions of what happened in Jerusalem in 587–86 BC, but they are true nonetheless.

With overwhelming imagery, the Lord's unrelenting response to Jerusalem's sin is displayed. It is furious, terrifying and devastating. No wonder then that, after verse 1, it's almost as if the poet cannot bear to mention God by name. Perhaps it's just too dreadful to acknowledge he is on the receiving end of God's judgment.

We feel this force in the chapter's cosmic movement, with the action channelling from God to creation. The Lord 'hurled down the splendour of Israel from heaven to earth' (2:1); the 'kingdom and its princes' are humbled 'down to the ground' (2:2). The tender and sacred language used to describe God's people – 'Daughter Zion' (2:1, 4); 'Daughter Judah' (2:2); 'his footstool' (2:1) – only serve to underline how catastrophic this is.

MAKING SENSE OF THE WRATH OF GOD

How do you feel about God's wrath? Our cultural instinct can be to resist any notion of God's anger, perhaps partly because it's virtually impossible not to conceive of it through the lens of our own experiences of human anger. Whilst we might sometimes speak of 'righteous anger', typically our anger is made up of impatience, selfishness and unreasonable hatred.

But we *have* to remember that God is altogether different to us. God is *not* like us. He is the Creator; we are creatures. He is both definitively different and beyond our full comprehension. God's wrath is an authentic expression of who he is. It's what happens when an unchanging God of holiness, love and justice comes into contact with evil, rebellion and sin.

These verses will not be easy to walk through, but as we wrestle with God's word, may he show us more of who he is.

Holy God, just and true, as we walk towards Jesus' cross this Lent, we cannot avoid your righteous wrath against sin. Help us to see you as you are, rather than as who we would like or imagine you to be. Give us eyes to see clearly, rather than through the lens of our own sinful experiences and personalities.

 Listen to 'O Lord the Clouds Are Gathering' by Graham Kendrick.

The Wrong Side
of the Warrior

Read Lamentations 2:5–8

A FIERCE WARRIOR

Throughout the Old Testament, God's people spoke of the Lord as 'a warrior' (see, for example, Exodus 15:3). His fierce protection of his people was seen most powerfully in the Exodus, where he overpowered the oppressive empire of Pharaoh. But now in Lamentations everything seems to have changed: God is fighting *against* his people, except it's not really much of a fight.

There is also a startling tension in this blunt language: 'He has multiplied mourning and lamentation for *Daughter Judah*' (2:5, 8; my italics). It's one thing to imagine God punishing enemies, but another thing altogether to conceive of God being 'like an enemy' to those whom he calls 'Daughter' (2:4–5). How do we handle this?

Evocative descriptions of the nation of Judah as 'Daughter Zion' run throughout the Old Testament, but no Bible book uses them as much as Lamentations. And strikingly, most of these references are here in chapter 2 (2:1, 4, 8, 10, 13, 18), interspersed with 'Daughter Judah' (2:2, 5) and 'Daughter Jerusalem' (2:13, 15). It's as if the poet *wants* us to feel the paradox of this situation.

DETERMINED TO DESTROY

Once again, the poet chooses to detail the way in which *God* has laid to waste the defences of Jerusalem. There is little doubt about God's power, with 'palaces' and 'strongholds' being swallowed up or destroyed (2:5). Like a special effects scene from a blockbuster movie, the city comes crashing down in slow motion all around us.

None of Israel's special privileges are spared: the 'place of meeting' and God's 'dwelling', the temple itself, is now laid waste, plucked up like a weed in a garden (2:6); the sound of joyful singing from Israel's festivals is no more (2:6), and instead the only noise is the enemy's shout of victory (2:7); the offices of king and priest have been humiliated (2:6). In a bitter twist, even the inner temple sanctuary, a place synonymous with God's presence, has been abandoned by him (2:7).

And it is all so unbearably *intentional*; the Lord is described as being 'determined' (2:8). Just as an architect carefully designs their construction plans, so the Lord stretches out a measuring line to get to work, but now it is to destroy rather than create (2:8). The walls and ramparts of Jerusalem, scenes of so many glorious moments in Israel's history, now crumble and cry out (2:8).

'LIKE AN ENEMY'

How do you feel about a God who can act 'like an enemy' (2:4–5)? For those of us whose faith rests in Jesus Christ this Lent, there is stunning mercy to be found in that little word 'like'. The full force of God's righteous anger against sin *is* a terrifying prospect for those outside of Jesus. But ultimately he is *not* an enemy to those who are 'in Christ'.

Yes, there is a chronological sense in which every Christian was once God's enemy (Romans 5:8–10); each of us was dead in our sins, following our own wayward desires, and therefore, by nature, 'deserving of wrath' (Ephesians 2:1–3). But on a hill outside Jerusalem, perhaps even on the original Mount Zion itself, the Son of God took the place of 'Daughter Zion'.

It takes a lot for someone to lay down their life for another person. Someone might choose to do so for a good person, but for an enemy? And in order to make that enemy a son or daughter?

The fierce judgment of God glimpsed in these verses only goes to magnify the outrageous nature of God's grace shown for us at the cross of Christ. As the apostle John writes, 'See what great love the Father has lavished on us, that we should be called children of God' (1 John 3:1). Today this Warrior now fights for you – raging against sin, death and the evil one.

 Listen to 'Lord of All' by Kristian Stanfill.

Day 11

Everything Is Lost

Read Lamentations 2:9–12

DON'T KNOW WHAT YOU'VE GOT 'TIL IT'S GONE

In Joni Mitchell's song 'Big Yellow Taxi', she sings the famous line, 'Don't it always seem to go: that you don't know what you've got 'til it's gone?' And as we turn to today's reading, there's no dressing it up: everything good seems to be gone for God's people. We're still reeling from the relentless and vivid descriptions of God's anger in 2:1–8, and yet there's hardly time to catch our breath before the camera pans around these smouldering ruins.

Notice how the narrative shifts from focusing on *God* as the subject ('He…') to focusing upon the impact of God's judgment upon the city, still personified as precious Daughter Zion ('her…'). Today, the writer particularly focuses on the *spiritual* loss resulting from Jerusalem's sin, lest we think this punishment is simply about broken buildings and destroyed walls.

God's glorious refrain to the nation of Israel, almost since the days of Abraham, had been one of gracious and affectionate privilege: 'he would be their God, and they would be his people' (see, for example, Genesis 17:7–8; Exodus 6:7; Leviticus 26:11–12). Now, those words seem a forgotten dream. *Everything* is lost.

PARADISE AND PRIVILEGE LOST

We see particularly in 2:9 how every spiritual privilege of God's people has been ferociously and decisively removed.

Firstly, the city gates, once a sign of security and welcome to God's pilgrim people (Psalm 118:20–24), have disintegrated into the ground.

Secondly, their king who sat on the historic throne of David is no more. As we'll explore later, King Zedekiah (who was only installed as a puppet king by Nebuchadnezzar a decade before) had fled Jerusalem, only to be captured, blinded and taken to Babylon. Brutally, the last thing he saw with his own eyes was the killing of his own sons, Jerusalem's 'princes'.

Thirdly, Israel's special identity, as the receivers of God's word, had now been ripped from them. By saying that 'the law is no more', our writer may mean that the books of the law had been stolen, along with the ark of the covenant. Just as those written words could no longer be accessed, so there will be no 'visions' for Jerusalem's 'prophets' either.

DYING OF A BROKEN HEART

Ironically, each of these spiritual consequences were symptomatic of the sins that had caused them. What God had taken *away* from his people was directly connected to what they had already tried to gain *without* him: they had turned elsewhere for security, so he had taken away their city walls; their kings had trusted in foreign powers, so now their own throne was vacant; they had abandoned and disobeyed God's words, and so now there was divine silence.

Who could fail to be moved by what we witness here? Our poet is certainly no distant bystander. Outwardly, he has wept so many tears that his eyes cannot handle it (2:11). Have you ever been so overcome with grief that the crying *hurts*? Inwardly, too, he is undone. His heart is broken and he is emotionally spent; it's as if his inner organs are poured out on the rubble-strewn floor (2:11). This was *his* people. These are the children of *his* nation lying faint in the streets, starved and helpless, drawing their last breath (2:11–12).

How serious do we think rebelling against God is? These verses show us that sin is not arbitrary. At its heart it is an act of spiritual revolution, as we seek to overthrow our Creator. But in his judgment, God devastatingly gives us what we ask for: life without every good thing. Do you see this in the world around us today? Pray we would lament what we have lost.

 Listen to *'Have Mercy'* by Sandra McCracken.

Day 12

City of Tears

Read Lamentations 2:13–15

UNHEALABLE WOUNDS

As many of us will know, words alone rarely make much difference in the midst of suffering. What we often need is *presence*. Someone *with* us; someone who wants to understand, cares for us and acknowledges our pain.

As we'll explore more later, the poet models this approach. Previously, the city had pleaded for anyone to 'look around and see. Is any suffering like my suffering?' (1:12). Now the poet directly addresses 'Daughter Jerusalem', showing her that, yes, she *is* 'seen'.

Sometimes we might try and offer a sufferer hope in the form of empathy: 'I remember when this happened to me…' or 'I can imagine it must feel like this…' But our poet knows Jerusalem's situation is beyond compare. Instead, only picture language can begin to capture her plight: 'Your wound is as deep as the sea' (2:13). Imagine the dark depths of the Pacific Ocean's Mariana Trench. With a wound that deep, the diagnosis is evident: 'Who can heal you?' (2:13).

UNSPEAKABLE LIES

Our poet has already lamented the loss of Jerusalem's leaders, but now he especially laments how her leaders misled the people. Singling out Judah's prophets, he calls their claims to speak for God 'false'; they were 'worthless' lies that sought popularity and an easy life (2:14).

The prophet Jeremiah also described the ministry of these prophets as deceitful: '"Peace, peace", they say, when there is no peace' (Jeremiah 6:13–14).

UNENVIABLE DOWNFALL

But it's not just the poet and the people themselves who feel the city's demise. As in 1:12, our poet references those who 'pass' by (2:15). Psalm 48 is cited here, so it's likely the poet means people from other nations. In many ways this song was a global testimony of God's goodness to Jerusalem: 'Great is the Lord, and most worthy of praise ... Beautiful in its loftiness, the joy of the whole earth ... is Mount Zion' (verses 1–2).

But how the mighty have fallen! The city that was the 'perfection of beauty' (2:15) is now a site of destruction that only invites mockery and prompts shock. People no longer visit this place and send home postcards about God's goodness to this nation. Instead, other nations shake their heads and whisper that something awful has happened here.

CHEAP GRACE

One test of whether we've truly 'seen' and felt Jerusalem's suffering is whether we too have heeded the warning of false 'prophets', who lull people into a false sense of security (2:13–14). During the rise of the Nazi regime, German pastor and theologian Dietrich Bonhoeffer criticised his national church for settling for a distorted faith that simply affirmed the political evils in their midst. He described how Christians often settle for 'cheap grace', such as 'the preaching of forgiveness without requiring repentance ... Cheap grace is grace ... without the cross, grace without Jesus Christ.'[7]

For Bonhoeffer, that message cost him his life – he was executed by the Nazis in 1945.

What are today's 'cheap grace' messages that might well please our ears and flatter our egos, but fatally distort God's truth? Maybe we reduce Christianity simply to 'insurance' for our deathbed? Or are we more interested in a church that is applauded by our cultural elites, than one set apart for the Lord? Do we prize 'sound doctrine' or a worship experience that meets our desires, but all the while keeping the Spirit's life-changing power at arm's length? When was the last time you allowed God to disagree with you?

 Listen to *'I Don't Have Much'* by Mission House (featuring Jess Ray and Taylor Leonhardt).

Day 13

God's Word Fulfilled

Read Lamentations 2:16–17

WHOSE DAY IS THIS?

Yesterday's passage described the shock of Jerusalem's neighbours as they witnessed her desperate state (2:15). Today, we see a less empathetic response. We already know Jerusalem's enemies laughed at her (1:7), crushing and prevailing over her (1:15, 16). Now, their gloating is plain to see: 'This is the day we have waited for; we have lived to see it' (2:16).

Were Jerusalem's enemies entitled to brag about her downfall? Just who was behind the fall of this city – the Babylonian empire or the Lord? This passage will take us deeper into some of the nuances of Jerusalem's destruction.

THE DAY PROUD ENEMIES LONGED FOR

Whilst Jerusalem's enemies now proudly declare they have 'swallowed her up' (2:16), this very same claim has already come from the lips of God (2:2). By using the same language, we're being shown that the boast of 2:16 smacks of human arrogance. These people are putting themselves in God's place.

Herein lies a tension that runs throughout these historical events. We know from 2 Kings 25 that the invasion and siege of Jerusalem was carried out by the Babylonian empire. And yet Babylon is never mentioned by name in Lamentations. It's as if the poet is resisting giving them that 'honour'. Instead, he has been making it clear that God is the one working to bring about his justice. How dare anyone else claim the 'glory' – this pride will be Babylon's downfall!

THE DAY MOSES LONG PROMISED

This truth is further underlined by the very next verse: 'The LORD has done what *he* planned' (2:17; my italics). But the language of 'fulfilled' and 'decreed' is not speaking of some secret, morbid intention God had to destroy Jerusalem. Instead, it connects us back to the public covenant that Israel had willingly entered into with God. As in 1:18, we're being reminded these horrific events were nothing less than the fulfilment of what God had promised *if* his people were unfaithful to him. There should be no surprises here.

We discover more about this covenant in the Old Testament book of Deuteronomy. God promised to lavish his blessing upon the people of Israel, providing them with a secure and prosperous land. But this covenant was dependent on Israel's faithful obedience (Deuteronomy 28:1–2). If they did not obey, God made it crystal clear that they would face the covenant 'curses' as he responded to their idolatry, disobedience and faithlessness (28:15). Over the following centuries, God indeed provided prophet after prophet to warn his people to keep that covenant – but to no avail.

Sadly, those covenant 'curses' (Deuteronomy 28–29) are eerily familiar as we read Lamentations: exile, judgment and suffering. God's people had even been warned of mockery by other nations and being considered a desolation (28:37). Whilst our initial reaction to Jerusalem's destruction might have been to think that God had been unfaithful to his people, we now see the opposite. These horrific events show God not reneging on his word but keeping his promise.

But even back in Deuteronomy there is also a glimmer of hope. These curses are punishment, but they have a restorative impact. They wake up an unfaithful and sin-sick people from their foolish stupor. Deuteronomy 30:1–10 speaks of God bringing a repentant people home. The apostle Paul tells us that Jesus' death bore these covenant curses as he hung 'on a tree' (Galatians 3:13, ESV). We can be redeemed – even from our self-seeking pride and Babylonian-esque arrogance.

 Listen to *'Father of Light'* by Celtic Worship.

Day 14

Good Grief

Read Lamentations 2:18–19

HONEST TO GOD

In the Johnny Cash biopic, *Walk the Line*, there's a fascinating scene where Cash's band is auditioning to a record executive. Cash chooses to sing a fairly bland gospel song about the peace of Jesus, but the executive stops him straight and poses Cash a question. If the singer were hit by a truck and lay dying in a gutter, but had time to sing one song, would he sing such 'a neat, shiny song'? Or would he sing something more raw and real? '*That's* the kind of song people want to hear,' says the executive. In response, Cash pens the gritty folk song 'Folsom Prison Blues', one of his most heralded works.[8]

In our Christian relationships and church services, how honest are we about life in this fallen world? Lamentations 2 has certainly been a brutal chapter. Having unflinchingly and candidly captured the experience of being under the Lord's judgment, our writer now begins to show us how we might respond. And it begins with an encouragement to face up to the reality of suffering.

SITTING IN THE SUFFERING

Don't miss how our poet sits *with* Jerusalem in her suffering. As Alianore Smith puts it, his posture is 'not as a detached observer, but as an active participant in her grief and pain.'[9]

Often our common response is instinctively to want to 'fix' another's suffering. Perhaps we do this by apportioning blame, or assembling a plan of action to change the situation. Of course, wanting to make the pain 'go away' is a natural reaction. But someone's suffering first needs to be acknowledged – and, in that sense, shared.

Another response may be to pull our eject cord and walk away from the sufferer. Perhaps we can't face the emotion? Maybe we feel awkward about being exposed to someone's vulnerability? Our reaction might even be connected to our own past experiences. Whilst we need to be self-aware and conscious of our own limits, there is also a place for sitting in someone's suffering.

WHERE ELSE CAN WE GO?

But as we find ourselves amidst dire straits, where can we turn? Listen again to the encouragement of the poet: 'pour out your heart like water in the presence of the Lord' (2:19).

When facing suffering, how easy it is to turn anywhere but to God – perhaps to self-help schemes, medication, entertainment, alcohol or drugs. Maybe we feel a whole range of 'negative' emotions towards God, be it blame, injustice or discomfort, which can then lead to a sense of guilt.

But the poet invites us to cry out to the Lord from our broken and imperfect hearts: 'let your tears flow like a river day and night; give yourself no relief, your eyes no rest' (2:18). This, ultimately, is faith. We can come to God in our grief, loss and despair. In the hospital waiting room. On the bathroom floor. After another morning unable to get out of bed. When we feel we can't share our darkest depths with anyone else, we *can* turn to the Lord.

Suffering does have potential to numb our senses over time, and sometimes that is self-protection. But how tragic it would be if we believed we weren't permitted to express our emotions before God.

Maybe sometimes we feel we can only bring 'neat, shiny' prayers to him? Your suffering – and the emotions it brings forth – are not too big, messy or raw to bring to God. Have you ever named your suffering in your prayers to him? Try doing that now.

 Listen to *'Now Is the Time for Tears'* by Charlie Peacock.

Day 15

Holy Discontent

Read Lamentations 2:20–22

A BITTER END

We may have breathed a sigh of relief seeing that today's reading is the last in this chapter! But as we read these verses, we soon see it's hardly a gentle conclusion. There are two especially striking aspects.

Firstly, these final verses capture how utterly unimaginable Jerusalem's fall was. And whilst our writer never explicitly questions whether this is right or just, he clearly feels it is almost outrageous that God would allow such horrors amongst his own people.

Secondly, as we grapple with such desperate events coming from God's hand, our poet now turns directly to God and expresses his lament. Yesterday's passage saw the poet encouraging his readers to cry out directly to the Lord (2:18–19). Now, he leads the way in doing just that. Rather than turning away from God in his suffering, he instead honestly addresses the Lord.

We'll consider both aspects in turn…

BEYOND BELIEF

We all have a sense that some things just should not be. Surely few people would disagree that the events in 2:20 belong in that category. Such events feel like they're ripping apart the moral fabric of life as we know it. But as the poet invites the people of Jerusalem to join him in lament, he also boldly urges God to 'look ... and consider' what is happening (2:20; cf. 1:11).

The poet leads us in lament with painful questions (2:20). These are effectively rhetorical, for no answer should be necessary. *Of course* mothers shouldn't be driven to such madness, hunger and despair that they eat their own children's bodies! *Of course* God's servants shouldn't be struck down in the most holy place! This is *beyond* belief. So has God broken the boundaries of his own moral order? Has he destroyed his own covenant? Is his very character now thrown into doubt?

AN UNCOMFORTABLE SOURCE

But *of course*, what is *most* horrifying here is facing up to the Lord's own will being behind these grim events. In fact, this conclusion is hard to miss; the chapter ends just as it began, with an explicit reference to the day of the Lord's anger (2:1, 22). Our writer has not hidden away from this conclusion throughout the chapter, but now he faces its brutal reality with poignant prose: just as God would summon his people to a feast day in Jerusalem, now he has summoned to the same city 'terrors on every side' (2:22).

As we discussed previously, though, these events are shocking but not surprising. In fact, they would have set off alarm bells for most Israelites! They were exactly what Moses had warned Israel about in the 'covenant curses' centuries before (Deuteronomy 28:52–57). *This* was the cost of disobedience.

This chapter ends with pointed questions and tear-drenched tension hanging in the air. No answers are given. No resolution is offered. Writer Mark Vroegop labels this aspect of lament as 'godly complaint'.[10] Rather than letting anger and bitterness isolate us or push us into stoic denial, we honestly bring our hearts to the Lord. God doesn't need our protection. Instead, we cast our questions upon the character of God: 'Whom have you ever treated like this?' (2:20).

 Listen to *'Darkness (Psalm 88)'* by Matt Searles.

Day 16

Rethinking Wrath

Read 1 Thessalonians 5:1–11

THINK ABOUT THE OPTICS…?

'The opposite of love is indifference.' So sang The Lumineers, the Denver-based folk rock band in their globally popular 2012 single, 'Stubborn Love'. It's a perceptive line that definitely makes you think. And as we look back on Lamentations 2, I wonder if it offers us surprising insight.

Over these past few days, our poet has brought us 'up close and personal' with the wrath of God. It's not been easy reading – and it's probably not what we're used to in our daily devotions either! Maybe you've wondered about the 'optics' of what you've read here? Perhaps you've thought God could do with hiring a decent press team to get himself out of this PR disaster?

Often, we instinctively think of God's wrath as opposed to his love, and so we feel we need to downplay wrath in order to highlight love. But what if that's a crucial mistake?

LOVE VERSUS WRATH?

The Croatian theologian Miroslav Volf used to reject the concept of God's anger, believing it to be 'unworthy' of God. But then, in the 1990s, his own people faced the utter terror and cruelty of the bloody war in former Yugoslavia. He suddenly found his views shifting in a surprising way: 'I came to think that I would have to rebel against a God who *wasn't* wrathful at the sight of the world's evil. God isn't wrathful in spite of being love. God is wrathful *because* God is love.'[11]

It's a remarkable perspective from the 'real world'. We might think that removing God's wrath leaves us with a more loving God, but Volf helps us see it has the opposite effect. In a world full of unpunished human evil, to remove God's wrath means we end up with a *less* loving God instead. That's because the opposite of love is not wrath, but an ugly and unholy indifference.

THERE WILL BE ANOTHER DAY

We know that Lamentations chiefly focuses on a particular kind of suffering: facing God's righteous judgment against sin. This fierce judgment is known as 'the day of [the LORD's] anger' (2:1, 22).

Yet, as in today's reading, the New Testament unavoidably picks up this same language to also describe a future day of judgment (see, for example, Romans 2:16; 2 Thessalonians 1:8–10; 2 Peter 3:10). Lamentations will even hint at a future day too (1:21–22; 4:21–22).

For Christians, we can rejoice that this particular future suffering will not be something we face, for Jesus has borne the punishment for our sin upon the cross: 'there is now no condemnation for those who are in Christ Jesus' (Romans 8:1). But Lamentations still helps us feel the terror of this future judgment for those who have not responded to Jesus' offer of rescue. While people might live like 'today' is all that matters, the Babylonian destruction of Jerusalem is a sobering reminder that rebelling against a holy God has future consequences.

Inevitably, there are huge challenges as we seek to understand and communicate God's wrath. For starters, it is virtually impossible not to think of God's anger in light of our own experiences of human anger. We might sometimes describe humans acting in 'righteous anger', but largely our anger is tainted by impatience, selfishness and other shortcomings. Yet God's wrath is not – it is a settled resolve, a loving reflex, a holy response.

> *How do you feel about the wrath of God being enacted against all evil, rebellion and idolatry? We might feel awkward about it or shuffle our feet, but the Bible writers seem to have no inhibitions about the goodness of God's wrath. When we appreciate the offence of sin and the reality of future judgment, then we are also amazed at the grace of the gospel.*
>
> ---
>
> Listen to *'Day of Judgement'* by Christ Church Mayfair.

Day 17

Behold the Man

Read Lamentations 3:1–9

THE FILLING IN THE MIDDLE

If Lamentations was a sandwich, this middle chapter is the all-important filling. It's the unavoidable centre of these five 'laments' – and, like a very generous sandwich, the filling is triple the size of the outer layers! Whilst it still follows the same A to Z 'acrostic' structure, now there are three verses for each letter of the Hebrew alphabet, rather than one! The poet is clearly saying, 'Look, this chapter *really* matters!'

We also notice a striking change in voice and perspective: 'I am the man…' (3:1). An individual now steps out of the shadows and into the spotlight.[12] No longer is the focus on a desolate city or a whole people living in sorrow, but on one person, a singular sufferer. This opening statement also makes the chapter stand out as it breaks the 'How…?!' pattern of the previous chapters (1:1; 2:1).

'I AM THE MAN'

Reading Lamentations so far has been like listening to a war correspondent evocatively reporting the ugly terrors they've seen 'on the ground'. But now we get something different: the microphone is passed over and we have first-hand testimony.

Instinctively we want to ask, 'Who is this man?' Is it just our poet giving his own personal perspective? Perhaps, but that would seem slightly egotistical for the book's longest and central chapter. Other commentators wonder if it's an imagined account of the famous prophet Jeremiah. He did minister during the Babylonian invasion – and certainly suffered (see Jeremiah 38). But whilst there are particular similarities to Jeremiah's own suffering, this personal account seems on an altogether different scale. Our eyes can't help being lifted beyond the events of 586 BC to something even greater…

THE 'I' OF THE STORM[13]

Before we consider the man's identity, we first need to acknowledge how right at the heart of Lamentations is not a description or a warning *about* God's wrath, but an account of someone facing God's wrath *themselves*: 'I am the man who has seen affliction by the rod of the LORD's wrath' (3:1). If we thought it was time to move on from God's strong anger against sin, we're quickly put right. A barrage of verses describe this individual's experience of God's hostility: 'He has driven me away … he has turned his hand against me … He has made my skin and my flesh grow old … He has besieged me' (3:2–5). Like previous chapters, it is unrelenting and fierce – but this time it's unquestionably personal.

Everything we've seen so far in Lamentations has told us that sinners deserve such judgment. This 'man' could be any citizen of Jerusalem in 586 BC. But just as one man stands at the centre of this book and faces God's wrath, so we know that one man stands at the centre of Scripture and faces God's holy wrath *for* us: Jesus Christ.

In fact, when Pilate has Jesus flogged before his crucifixion, he even says, 'Here is the man!' (John 19:5). Looking at these verses from the standpoint of the whole of Scripture, we see Jesus Christ clearly. He was made to dwell in darkness (Lamentations 3:2, 6). He was forsaken spiritually (3:8). He was then placed with those long dead (3:6), his tomb sealed with a stone (3:9).

Sometimes in Lent, we can become unhealthily focused on ourselves: our own sin, mortality and brokenness. But our prayer should be for Jesus to be magnified in the eyes of our weak and broken hearts. Why not reread today's verses imagining Jesus upon the cross. Pray the Spirit would fill our gaze with Jesus this Lent.

 Listen to *'Man of Sorrows'* by Steffany Gretzinger.

How Low Can You Go?

Read Lamentations 3:10–20

HUNTED

As we started to see yesterday, this chapter begins with a tangibly unpleasant, first-person account of suffering at the hands of a seeming oppressor. But the desperate reality behind these verses is that it's God who is active here.

Christopher Wright notes how we're often familiar with the Old Testament's descriptions of God as a shepherd who defends his people from wild beasts. Less familiar are portrayals of God like one of those dangerous beasts (3:10–11). Even the protective weaponry of the shepherd's bow is now used by God against the man (3:12);[14] he is pierced to the very heart (3:13).

No wonder that God's covenant name (captured in our English translations as 'the LORD') is not mentioned between 3:1 and 3:18. This absence captures a sense of the sufferer struggling to process just how far things have fallen.

PRONE TO WANDER

The horrific imagery builds up cumulatively. There is brutal taunting and mockery (3:14). 'Bitter herbs' and 'gall', often associated with acute sorrow, are this individual's forced diet (3:15). Tellingly, these substances were also synonymous with being consequences of sinful idolatry – as in the covenant curses of Deuteronomy 29:18. The man's teeth are then broken, perhaps as he is forced to eat gravel as a punishment, or from being literally trampled into the dust (3:16).

What a fate. It is painfully palpable. The man is 'deprived of peace', literally 'shalom', and has 'forgotten what prosperity [goodness] is' (3:17). As low points go, you'd struggle to get much lower. It is the definition of being 'hope-less'.

Given all of this, it's unsurprising that as we reach the end of today's passage, the sufferer recalls how these experiences fill his mind (the language of 'remembering' is used twice, 3:19–20). Specifically, he remembers his 'affliction' and 'wandering', a pairing that mirrors Jerusalem's fate of exile in 1:7. But 'wandering' also has a powerful double meaning. God's people *were* forced to wander far from home when exiled to Babylon, but this happened *because* their hearts first wandered from the Lord. It's a reminder that this is the testimony of someone not just facing immeasurable suffering, but one who knows they have been unfaithful to the sacred relationship for which they were created. As such, not only is his body broken, but his soul is downcast (3:20).

DO YOU KNOW THIS MAN?

We recognise from the eyewitness accounts of the Gospels that this man's story bears powerful resemblance to Jesus' story. *He* is the man who was seized by those lying in wait for him as he prayed in Gethsemane (3:10–11; cf. Matthew 26:48–51). *He* is the man who was given gall to drink before he was hoisted upon a cross (3:15; cf. Matthew 27:33–34). Though Jesus is the true king of the earth, *his* splendour was taken away as he was stripped and given a scarlet robe (3:18; cf. Matthew 27:28–29). *He* is the man who was mocked mercilessly with sarcastic 'reverence' and a crown of thorns (3:14; cf. Matthew 27:29). Finally, *he* was pierced, both outwardly in the brutality of crucifixion, but also inwardly as he took the punishment for our rebellion (3:13; cf. Matthew 27:35, 46).

> *All of us deserve to stand where the man of Lamentations 3 stands; every day we each 'wander' away from God, in thought, word and deed. But Jesus Christ willingly stood in our place. Give thanks for this 'man' who took our sentence and walked to the cross.*
>
> ---
>
> Listen to *'Come Thou Fount (I Will Sing)'* by Chris Tomlin.

New Even on the Darkest Morning

Read Lamentations 3:21–24

FAMILIAR VERSES; UNFAMILIAR PLACE

If there were any verses from Lamentations that you knew before beginning this devotional, my guess would be they're the following from today's passage: 'Because of the LORD's great love we are not consumed, for his compassions never fail. They are new every morning; great is your faithfulness' (3:22–23).

Recognise them? Thought so. Perhaps you've seen them printed on some Christian kids' stationery, alongside a yellow smiley face, or featured in some beautifully outlined letter art. The problem is that when we lift these verses out of context, we have a tendency to miss the significance of what they're actually saying. We think their natural habitat is a world where 'all is well' and the sun is shining. Thankfully, the good news is they're more at home in a quite different place – and that changes everything.

WHERE HOPE IS FOUND

Do you notice the movement from 3:20 to 3:21? First, the poet 'remembers' his circumstance and so his soul is downcast. He stands in the ruins of a smoking Jerusalem facing the judgment of God. But then the shift happens. There is a 'calling to mind', a deliberate act of the will. Barry Webb puts it like this:

> '[It] is deliberate; a choice the sufferer has made. It is in this choice that hope is reborn. But it is clear that something more is involved than a determined change to a more positive frame of mind, as though hope had been conjured up out of thin air by a sheer act of the will. The substance for it resides not so much in the choice itself as in what has been chosen.'[15]

What follows is a staggering confession of faith, featuring some of the Old Testament's key words describing God's covenant with his people: 'great love … compassion … faithfulness'.

It's no coincidence that all these words feature in the great covenantal declaration of God's character in Exodus 34:6. Evidently the poet knew these verses like the back of his hand, and yet fascinatingly he doesn't just recite them. Instead, as he calls them to mind, there is fresh beauty, wonder and joy. And whilst the words are uniquely his own they are also inclusive ('we are not consumed', 3:22).

STEADFAST LOVE IN THE RUINS

Remember that these are not words spoken from some perfectly curated living room or beach vista. They come from the ruins of a beloved city. A deathly silence hangs over this place, broken only by cries of anguish from survivors. Does that seem odd to you?

But a biblical hope is grounded not in what we see or feel, but in the object of our trust, the character of God (Hebrews 11:1). Therefore it can endure suffering and is not dependent on a change of circumstance.

In *The Jesus Storybook Bible*, Sally Lloyd-Jones wonderfully describes God's covenant love as his 'Never Stopping, Never Giving Up,

Unbreaking, Always and Forever Love'.[16] With every new day, God's grace is available as we turn our hearts to him, and this mercy always leads us to God himself: 'The LORD is my portion' (Lamentations 3:24).

What soundbites or phrases does our culture 'call to mind' when someone faces suffering? What have you heard people say, write or post when someone goes through a hard time? Instead, what might it look like for you to follow the poet's example in 3:21? How do you find clinging to God's character, even when everything else feels hopeless?

 Listen to *'Morning by Morning (I Will Trust)'* by Pat Barrett (featuring Mack Brock).

Day 20

Hope in the Dust

Read Lamentations 3:25–30

WAITING IN THE DARK

The writer Barbara Brown Taylor makes a telling observation about the twenty-first-century Western church:

> *One thing that had always troubled me was the way people disappeared from the church when their lives were breaking down ... I was sorry that the church did not strike these wounded souls as the place where they could bring the dark fruits of their equally dark nights.*[17]

I'm sure there's lots going on underneath Taylor's remark. However, when lives are 'breaking down', one of Lamentations' offerings for 'wounded souls' is perhaps to help us develop the lost Christian discipline of waiting.

How have you found waiting recently? In the queue at the coffee shop? For that item you ordered online only yesterday? Or 'on hold' to the doctors trying to book an appointment?

Of course, those things may feel fairly superficial 'first-world problems', but what about when our waiting has no real end in sight? When we're desperately hoping to conceive? When another job application goes unanswered? When there's no sign on the horizon of that partner we so desperately long for? As one writer puts it, waiting is like waking up in the movie *Groundhog Day*, where every 'today' just feels like yesterday.[18]

LEARNING TO WAIT

Right at the heart of Lamentations is the repeated language of waiting (3:24, 26). In fact, the language of hoping, bearing a yoke and sitting alone is all connected to the same idea (3:25–28). And, perhaps much to the surprise of our cultural hang-up with delays, the poet portrays waiting as 'good'!

If we were reading the original Hebrew, we'd notice that each verse in 3:25–27 begins with the word 'good'. Not only is it 'good to wait quietly' for the Lord (3:26), but 'the LORD is good' to those who wait for him (3:25). It is worth just pausing and reflecting on this statement, given everything we've seen over the last twenty days. The Lord is good?!

Clearly the poet's 'calling to mind' in 3:21 has had a radical impact. Suddenly the desperate scenes of a decimated Jerusalem are not at the forefront of the poet's mind. It's not that he's escaped his city and gone off on some spiritual retreat. Rather, in the *midst* of suffering and pain, he is clinging to something else. If God is good, then his promises must be true. There must be something beyond what we can see.

WHERE OUR HEARTS HOPE

The pastor and writer Tim Keller, who died of pancreatic cancer in 2023, wrote powerfully about waiting through suffering. Reflecting on Psalm 42 and the way the psalmist analyses his own hopes, Keller imagines a subsequent conversation with our hearts:

We may hear our hearts say, 'It's hopeless!' but we should argue back. We should say, 'Well, that depends what you were hoping in. Was that the right thing to put so much hope in?'[19]

Of course, this is not easy. In fact, quite the opposite! It's intrinsically painful and uncomfortable. It is a humbling 'yoke' (Lamentations 3:27) as we find ourselves quietly facing the dust (3:26, 28–29).

In what ways are you feeling the discomfort of waiting today? In a world of tears, learning to wait is critical for resilient disciples. But perhaps we often project a vision of life where the aspirational norm is for everything to be fine all the time? Tragically, this leaves those facing suffering with nowhere to call home, and we miss out on seeing the 'good' sanctifying work that God wants to do in us as we wait.

 Listen to *'I Will Wait for You (Psalm 130)'* by Shane & Shane.

Wrestling with Sovereign Grace

Read Lamentations 3:31–39

LIFE THROUGH THE LENS OF GOD'S LOVE

Sometimes life is just hard and there are no easy answers. As we've seen, our poet probably knows this better than most. And yet despite his circumstances, he begins today with a bold declaration of a hopeful future: '*For* no one is cast off by the Lord forever' (3:31; my italics). As we imagine our poet sat amidst the ruins of Jerusalem, we might wonder how he can be so confident?

But today's passage is like a crash course in seeing life through the character of God. We already know he intentionally calls this to mind (3:21–23). Now, we witness him mentally and emotionally battling to see his experiences through the lens of God's 'unfailing love' (3:32; as in 3:22). In other words, this is not wishful thinking or simply an optimistic personality. The poet's hope comes solely from the revealed character and promises of God.

When Moses laid out the covenant blessings and curses, one remarkable promise flowing out of God's character was that he would show mercy to a repentant exiled remnant (Deuteronomy 30:1–11). Our poet is articulating nothing that hasn't already been revealed.

DOES GOD DELIGHT IN JUDGMENT?

But as we reach 3:33, it's natural to question how this fits with everything in Lamentations so far. How can the poet say God has not 'willingly' brought affliction? The NIV translation of 3:33 is perhaps slightly misleading. The emphasis is less a statement of God's intentionality and more about capturing his heart or priority. A better translation could be: 'His heart is not in bringing suffering.' Ezekiel likewise recounts how the Lord takes 'no pleasure in the death of the wicked' (Ezekiel 33:11).

It's evident that as the poet wrestles with this situation, he is seeking to use his limited words to capture something quite profound about God. In the midst of the devastation in Jerusalem, God's character *cannot* have changed. Therefore, it *must* still be legitimate to proclaim that the Lord is *for* justice, righteousness and the dignity of the oppressed.

In other words, these horrendous events are *not* the result of God disregarding his own standards of justice and righteousness. The poet can declare the 'justice' of Jerusalem's punishment, whilst *also* expecting this justice to be grounds for believing the current state of affairs won't go on forever.

THREE BIG ASKS

Finally, in 3:37–39, our poet zooms out from Jerusalem and offers three rhetorical questions to remind us of our place on the canvas of our sovereign God. As the Creator of all things, only God can have 'decreed' what has occurred in Jerusalem. Therefore only God can guarantee the future of his people.

Naturally that raises *why* God would ordain evil. But the 'calamities' in 3:38 are not speaking of moral evil. Instead, the likes of suffering, defeat and death – even the destruction of a 400-year-old holy temple

– can be God's means of bringing about his good plans, including his justice upon moral evil. The poet concludes by gently putting us in our place: 'Why should the living complain when punished for their sins?' (3:39; cf. Romans 9:19–20). In other words, any judgment is *always* deserved – and the presence of life itself is a gift of God's grace.

> *Do you view your life through the lens of God's gracious character? There are always grounds for hope for those who live in rhythms of repentance and trust in God's promises – and yet it's not easy. Sometimes we are given the privilege of seeing how God has worked a situation for our good, but for much of life that might not be the case. Instead, 'we live by faith, not by sight' (2 Corinthians 5:7). This does take some inner wrestling – and lots of waiting.*
>
> ---
>
> Listen to 'The Valley' by Ellie Holcomb.

Day 22

Time to Turn

Read Lamentations 3:40–48

RESISTING SPIRITUAL ENTITLEMENT

American psychologist Jean Twenge says we live in an 'age of entitlement', from narcissistic parenting to employees' expectations of office perks. And, of course, if entitlement culture is the air we breathe, we'd be wise to consider its impact upon church too. Today, our poet offers us a refreshing solution of 'entitlement-resistance'.

LET US PRAY

With the frank assessment of 3:39 still on the tip of his tongue, our poet invites us first to whole-hearted self-examination, then to repentance, and then to contrite confession ('Let us… let us… let us…', 3:40–41).

The opening half of 3:42 begins emphatically in the Hebrew: 'We, we, have sinned and rebelled…' And there is clearly not even a whiff of presumption here. It's as if the poet hits a spiritual brick wall: '… and you, you, have not forgiven'. Given the glorious declaration of God's compassion in 3:21–27, does this mean God's character has changed? Has the poet lost confidence in the mercy of God? Is there a limit to God's grace?

But 3:42 could also be translated as 'you did not forgive'. In other words, the crucial point isn't God still choosing not to forgive, but rather that he has not overlooked their rebellion. That's why Jerusalem now lies in ruins. There is an inevitability about God's judgment upon sin that the poet knows we must face up to.

COVER STORY

With dramatic visual language, the poet then captures the felt experience of being spiritually separated from the Lord. God has covered himself with 'anger' and 'a cloud' (3:43–44). Whilst the 'covering' of the ark of the covenant was where God provided atonement for sin, and the guiding pillar of cloud assured Israel of God's presence, now, devastatingly, these 'coverings' speak of anger and absence.

And whilst the poet has shown contrition and repentance, that doesn't stop him from poetically lamenting the horror of his situation. As the ESV translation of 3:47 puts it, '*panic* and *pitfall* have come upon us, *devastation* and *destruction*' (my italics). Only tears could be the appropriate response (3:48). And yet by repeatedly emphasising who he is speaking to ('you… you… you…', 3:43–45), it's clear the poet is praying to the covenant Lord. In other words, though God's wrath is unquestionable, hope lies in a God who hears.

WE NEVER GRADUATE FROM REPENTANCE

Whilst there is much to lament in our world, Lamentations models that Christians never graduate from personal confession of sin. Yes, it's right to cry out at the selfish and wicked actions of others. Yes, it's fitting to plead for justice when we or others are being mistreated. But we always do so from a place of humble contrition for our own sin. The theologian Mike Ovey suggested the benchmark of true repentance is whether we only repent of what our culture says is offensive, or whether we are also ready to repent of that which God says is wrong.[20]

Every sin is a departure from walking towards God – it needs a change of direction. Biblically, we can't speak about forgiveness without speaking about repentance – they go hand in hand. If we aren't walking in rhythms of repentance, then we're not walking in forgiveness.

The practice of daily self-examination, confession and repentance is a precious Christian rhythm. King David prayed, 'Search me, God, and know my heart; test me and know my anxious thoughts. See if there is any offensive way in me, and lead me in the way everlasting' (Psalm 139:23–24). Of course, the human heart is more than capable of deceiving itself, so we must pray for soft hearts that are ready to be convicted by God's Spirit every day – including through the prods of others. But we also need to give time and space to examine, repent and confess.

 Listen to 'My Portion' by Advent Birmingham (featuring Zac Hicks).

Day 23

The Tracks of Our Tears

Read Lamentations 3:49–57

UNCEASING TEARS

Have you thought much about tears? Tears have been a regular occurrence in Lamentations. Just as the city has wept (1:16), so the poet has wept (2:11, 18). Now, this particular suffering man weeps as well.

It is sometimes tempting to shy away from tears. We might hold back our own tears, or turn our face away when we see the tears of others. But the man speaking is totally *unashamed* of his own tears. Some even translate these verses as the man saying he's wept more tears than 'all the women of the city' (3:51).

Strikingly, he pledges to weep *until* things change (3:50). A few years ago, it was popular for Christians to wear bracelets with the acronym P.U.S.H., meaning 'Pray Until Something Happens'. Well, this individual models L.U.S.H.: 'Lament Until Something Happens'. Weeping and crying is an entirely understandable and appropriate reaction to life in this broken world. But we also lament now because we believe this world won't be broken forever, and we long for that day to come. We cry both because things *aren't* ok, and because we know one day everything will be ok.

THE PITS

Note the water imagery throughout today's passage. First are the individual's unceasing tears (3:49), but then we have a graphic description of the man being thrown into a pit with deathly waters closing over his head (3:53–54).

If we're familiar with the fate of the prophet Jeremiah, then at first glance we might assume this is a poetic account of his life. During Jeremiah's ministry, he was thrown into a pit by those who resisted his message (Jeremiah 38:1–6). Yet, we're specifically told that pit was only full of mud, *not* water (38:6).

Is there more going on here? As well as being used to describe a water storage well, the Hebrew word translated as 'pit' (Lamentations 3:53, 55) was associated with being a place of imprisonment or a grave. The dramatic salvation language of 3:55–57 also seems to be on a different scale to Jeremiah being lifted from a well with worn-out rags (Jeremiah 38:11–13). A greater rescue seems to be anticipated here; it is the covenant God, the Lord, who hears the man's plea, comes near and raises him from the grip of death.

THE GOD WHO COMES NEAR

We have already seen prophetic glimpses of the work of Jesus throughout this chapter. And so if Lamentations 3:1–19 prefigured Jesus' crucifixion, then surely the dramatic rescue of today's passage foreshadows Jesus' resurrection and ascension. Though he was 'delivered over to death for our sins', he was not abandoned to the grave (Romans 4:25). Rather, he was raised to life by the Father in the power of the Spirit (8:11). And because of that 'rescue', he is the only one who can rescue us from death.

Our tears in this world of sin, suffering and death might feel unceasing. But today we can take heart because we have a God who comes near (3:57). He sees (3:50) and hears (3:56). And better than just looking down from heaven (3:50), our God actually comes down and enters the depths of the pit himself. As we look forward to Easter, when we celebrate Jesus being raised from death in resurrection glory, today let's celebrate that we too can receive life and relief from the covenant Lord.

 Listen to *'Son of Suffering'* by The Worship Initiative.

Every Wrong Righted

Read Lamentations 3:58–66

GOD OF JUSTICE

We all long for a day when justice is delivered and 'things are put right'. Many people are giving their time to highlighting injustices and rallying others to see them 'put right'. Sadly, each of us will have our own examples of where injustice has led to pain, unrest and distrust.

The poet concludes his third lament with a passionate cry for 'vengeance' to be delivered to God's people (3:60). Often we associate vengeance with revenge, but that is a misstep. Lament and justice go hand in hand. We lament because of injustice, and we lament by longing for justice.

LEGAL DEFENCE

Much of Lamentations has wrestled with God justly punishing his people for their sin, but today our poet explores how justice must also be enacted against those who have laid Jerusalem low. Though Judah's punishment at the hands of the Babylonian army was deserved (see, for example, 3:40–42), the Babylonians are also culpable for their blood-thirsty and unrelenting mistreatment of God's people.

And as the poet pleads to God 'from the depths of the pit' (3:55), a place of seeming helplessness, he nevertheless testifies of God's action on his behalf: 'You, Lord, took up my case; you redeemed my life' (3:58). Notice that God doesn't just speak platitudes. He actually takes up our cause. Interestingly, the language in 3:58 is inherently legal. God is his people's advocate and defender. He is the one who acts to 'redeem', a legal term meaning to be bought back from slavey, liberated and have life restored.

NOTHING HIDDEN FROM HIM

Justice requires a God who sees (3:59–60) and hears (3:61), even when cruel threats and plans are spoken quietly and in secret (3:62). When backs are turned, when the cameras are off and when official minutes are no longer being taken, God still sees and hears. This is the grounds for the poet asking God to act, because he knows that God has witnessed everything: 'pay them back … put a veil over … may your curse be on them … pursue them …' (3:64–66).

Just as the destruction of Jerusalem was part of the 'covenant curses' for Judah's disobedience (Deuteronomy 27–28), now our poet longs for what he believes the nations deserve. And he uses the same word, 'pursue', to capture this longing. Where the likes of Babylon once 'pursued' Israel (Lamentations 1:3, 6; 3:43), now the poet urges God to enact his wrath by 'pursuing' the enemies of his people (3:66).

There is an understanding here that our own sin doesn't justify someone else's sin. The judgment that has fallen upon God's people doesn't disqualify them from receiving justice for what has been done to them. As sinful people, yes, we plead for justice with a humility and contrition that acknowledges we are far from perfect. But equally that doesn't mean we cannot plead!

Can you think of present instances where God's people are being treated by others with a 'depth of … vengeance' (3:60)? Though Christians are commanded not to repay evil for evil themselves (Romans 12:14–18), we are still to cry out for God to vindicate his people. He is a God of justice, and so we 'leave room for God's wrath' by longing for that day of justice (Romans 12:19–21). But as those who are 'in Christ' plead for justice, our posture is never one of pride or superiority – we know we too deserved the 'curse' of God's judgment ourselves.

 Listen to *'In Labor All Creation Groans'* by Bifrost Arts.

Day 25

The Man Who Set His Face

Read Luke 19:28–44

THE MAN WHO CHANGES EVERYTHING

As we take a day to pause after Lamentations 3, we focus again on the chapter's central character, 'the man' (3:1). It is his presence that seems to have caused the first rays of sunrise to peek through the ruins of this forsaken city. Stepping out from the shadows of the city, it is he who is facing the storm of the Lord's wrath (3:1) – bringing covenant hope to this city.

We have already reflected on how this man gives us a glimpse of Jesus Christ. Today, we will trace Jesus' role as the man who walked towards Jerusalem, rather than away from it.

FACE LIKE FLINT

In Luke's Gospel, Jesus' journey to Jerusalem takes up nine of the twenty-four chapters. It is a slow and steady journey, filled with detail and teaching, but resolute none the less. And it begins with a clear headline in the narrative: 'He set his face to go to Jerusalem' (Luke 9:51, ESV).

Luke's language is an allusion to Isaiah's prophecy about the promised Suffering Servant. In particular, this character is described as having a face 'set ... like a flint' (50:7). Flint is hard, one of the toughest rocks readily found in Israel. This servant was absolutely resolved to bring God's salvation.

The people of Israel were certainly hoping for a king to return to their city and bring God's victory and salvation. But as Jesus set his face for Jerusalem, he knew something else was needed first: a death like no other (Luke 18:31–33).

WAITING FOR EXILE'S END

As twenty-first-century readers, we perhaps don't feel the significance of Israel's exile to Babylon. It was such a cataclysmic event that Matthew uses it as one of only three defining time-markers – alongside the lives of Abraham and David – in his genealogy of Jesus (1:11–12). But whilst Matthew refers to exile beginning, he never mentions it ending.

Yes, some people had returned from Babylon. The Persians' defeat of the Babylonians had seen to that. But as we see in Ezra and Nehemiah, that return was nothing special. People were still waiting for a spiritual end to exile.

That's why people were coming to John the Baptist in repentance and seeking forgiveness (Mark 1:4). That's why old Simeon was still awaiting Israel's 'consolation' or comfort (Luke 2:25; cf. Isaiah 40:1). Just as the whole of humanity had been in a cosmic exile since Genesis 3, many in Jerusalem longed for someone who would deal with their sin once and for all.

DEATH OUTSIDE THE CITY

So when Jesus willingly entered into Jerusalem, we see there is hope for exiled hearts. The second Adam, a new Israel, a perfect Son is here! And more than that, his sin-bearing, curse-facing death will restore people back to God. In the most famous of Isaiah's other 'servant songs', we're told this man of suffering faces the 'punishment that brought us peace' (53:3–5).

Even the decision to crucify Jesus outside the city was a reminder that God was at work. On the Day of Atonement, bulls and goats were sacrificed 'outside the camp' to indicate they had taken on the people's sin (Leviticus 16:27; Numbers 19:3). Now, Jesus had become the ultimate sacrifice for sin.

Are there areas of your life where you still feel disconnected or distant from God? How does seeing Jesus as the man who set his face to Jerusalem – willingly bearing our sin and bringing an end to our spiritual exile – bring hope and healing to those areas?

 Listen to *'No One Ever Cared for Me Like Jesus'* by Steffany Gretzinger.

Day 26

Postcards from Hell

Read Lamentations 4:1–5

VOYEURS OF HORROR

In a world of twenty-four-hour news cycles, viral trends and shortening attention spans, psychological experts have begun to talk about 'crisis fatigue'. An ever-changing media diet of 'bad news stories' is apparently leaving us with higher rates of apathy, feelings of helplessness, escapism tendencies and a lack of empathy. Maybe part of the value of Lamentations is helping us relearn how to respond to suffering without quick fixes, easy answers and social media's 'flavour of the month' crisis signalling.

We've just journeyed to the hope-filled middle point of Lamentations, but as we work our way back out to the wild edges, we again face up to the grim consequences of Jerusalem's rebellion. Once more, there is a change of voice; we've previously focused on 'she', 'he' and 'I', but now we move to 'they'. Gone is the personal torment of chapter 3, and instead we find a more detached tone – with a desperate cross-section of life in this city of judgment.

This is the grim reality after the war correspondents have packed their bags, found their passports and rushed home. This is the 'new normal'.

WORTHLESS

The opening lines immediately give a sense of degradation. We recognise the familiar cry of exasperation, 'How...?!' (4:1; cf. 1:1

and 2:1), but this time it draws our attention to the discarded gold of a once glorious city. We're being reminded Jerusalem is now a place where even the most precious objects have little significance. 'Sacred gems', which once presumably had pride of place in the temple itself, now just lie 'scattered' on the streets (4:1).

But these abandoned stones actually tell an even more brutal story. Without missing a beat, the poet likens them to God's people. Once precious, they are now seemingly forsaken; once cherished, they are now just disposable 'pots of clay' (4:2).

HEARTLESS

This chapter will particularly show us how sin has left its mark not just on people's everyday lives, but upon their hearts too. These divine image-bearers are now shattered and defiled, bearing little resemblance to the people God created them to be.

The poet painfully contrasts the city residents with the wild beasts that roam these ruins. Whilst the jackals nurse their young, sin has left the people of Jerusalem 'heartless', less than human. They have become 'like ostriches in the desert' (4:3), often considered careless for leaving their eggs on the ground, perhaps even crushing them with their own feet. These people no longer have the will or capacity to care for and feed their own (4:4).

This is a desperate place to be. Those who had feasted on luxuries now find themselves hunting for scraps in the street; bodies that once were decorated in resplendent purple now lie discarded and blackened on 'ash heaps' (4:5).

The degradation of sin is not just something we experience outwardly; it occurs inwardly as well. As God gives us over to our choices, our values and sense of moral order are often distorted. We no longer think, feel and act as we ought. It's a horrific picture, and a reminder that none of us are immune to our sinful choices impacting us in ways beyond which we might see.

 Listen to *'Lord Have Mercy (For What We Have Done)'* by Matt Boswell and Matt Papa.

Depths of Darkness

Read Lamentations 4:6–10

SODOM 2.0

As we journey through this cross-section of life in Jerusalem, we'll notice the particular nature of Jerusalem's suffering. This is a city under siege, with the Babylonians inflicting a merciless war of attrition.

But as with each chapter in this book, the poet leaves us with no 'wriggle room' as to his verdict for why we're here: these events are due 'punishment' (4:6). However, if we weren't yet convinced of how seriously God views Jerusalem's sin, one phrase today should stop us in our tracks: 'greater than that of Sodom' (4:6).

Back in Genesis, Sodom was known as a city of wickedness (Genesis 18:20). Despite Abraham's pleading, Sodom's evil was exposed when its people tried to rape the two angelic messengers God sent to Abraham's nephew, Lot (19:1, 5). Consequently, God's holy anger burned against the city and it was destroyed. All that was left of Sodom was its legacy as a byword for sin and destruction.

And yet this comparison was not uncharted territory for Jerusalem. Moses had explicitly warned the people of Israel that if they went their 'own way', God's curse would fall upon them, 'like the destruction of Sodom …' (Deuteronomy 29:19, 23). The red warning light had already been flashing. Now it had come to pass...

LIFE WITHOUT TECHNICOLOUR

The power of the poetry in Lamentations is the way it engages our imaginations and emotions. Here we see haunting descriptions of Jerusalem as having all colour drained from it.

Previously, the gold decor had been dulled and the royal purple garments of Jerusalem's elite had been replaced by blackened ash (4:1, 5). Today, we see this devastating reversal in Jerusalem's 'princes', probably the city's nobles and dignitaries. Once displaying their privilege with glowing pale skin, ruby-like complexion and the healthy shine of lapis lazuli stone, now they have been left dark, shrivelled and unrecognisable (4:7–8). Privilege and wealth are no protection against God's judgment.

BEYOND BLEAK

Gradually, the awful reality of siege warfare hits home. Even a bloody death would be better than this slow and endless massacre of famine (4:9). We especially reel back as we read 4:10. It's beyond our imaginations that a child could be food for her mother's cooking. Instinctively, we hope it's some figurative imagery of hopelessness – but tragically siege warfare was known to cause such horrific acts. Again, this is what Moses had already foreseen if God's people rebelled (Deuteronomy 28:53–57).

As twenty-first-century Christian readers, these descriptions should act as warning sirens, unsettling us from our ease with sin. Do we see sin as this destructive? It is not an arbitrary offence to be punished, but a seeping oil leak that spreads and spoils, devastating all around it. How can we be ambivalent to such a loss of everything good, beautiful and true?

To compare Jerusalem with Sodom, which exemplified the ultimate degradation of humanity throughout the Old Testament, was a stinging criticism. Yet it was a comparison that Jesus himself made as he sent out his apostles to the 'lost sheep of Israel' (Matthew 10:5, 15). And all sin is similarly degrading. Do we think like this each day, as we choose a life without God in the 'everyday moments' of our existence?

 Listen to *The Year of the Locust* by Andrew Osenga.

Day 28

Unthinkable for the Unsinkable

Read Lamentations 4:11–16

WHEN THE UNTHINKABLE HAPPENS

'There is no danger that Titanic will sink. The boat is unsinkable and nothing but inconvenience will be suffered by the passengers.'

Those were the infamous words of Phillip Franklin, the vice-president of the White Star Line shipping company in 1912. The rest, as they say, is history.

But if it was unthinkable that the mighty *Titanic* might sink, how much more was it inconceivable that blessed Jerusalem might fall. After all, was this not God's people and God's city?! And yet our poet's conclusion is consistent with each chapter: it is the Lord who has poured out his fierce anger upon his precious Zion (4:11).

This wasn't just a shock to God's people. This was a headline that reverberated around the nations of the world (4:12). In a cruel twist, Israel had been called to be a light for the nations, yet now the nations were talking about Jerusalem's shameful plight.

LEADERSHIP FAILURE

Having shown us the wide-angle, global scale of astonishment at Jerusalem's fall, our poet now drills down deep into a specific cause that's not yet been made explicit in Lamentations: 'But it happened because of the sins of her prophets, and the iniquities of her priests' (4:13).

Here we have a laser-focused diagnosis, with the poet portioning particular blame upon Jerusalem's spiritual leaders. The 'prophets' were those called to lead God's people and call them back to repentance. The priests were those who would administer the temple worship and sacrificial rhythms. Both had failed to undertake their roles and as such God's people were desperately vulnerable.

It's not quite clear what the poet means by the shedding and defilement of blood (4:13–14). This may be a reference to idolatrous practices, or it may be these leaders had partaken in violent corruption. We certainly know the prophet Jeremiah faced physical attacks from temple workers (Jeremiah 18:18; 20:1–12).

But, with bitter irony, God's judgment upon the prophets and priests actually embodies the very charge for which they were guilty: the prophetic 'seers' now grope around as if blind; the priests, whose role was to remind people of their need for purifying atonement, are now themselves defiled and shunned as 'unclean'.

COMPLACENCY AT THE HELM

In the wake of the *Titanic*'s sinking, there were various reports of leadership failure. Some claimed the ship's skipper steered the boat too fast in the iceberg-heavy waters of the North Atlantic; others pointed to the ship's wireless operator ignoring a radio warning of icebergs from a nearby ship; more recently scientists have tested rivets from the wreck and theorised the ship's builders used cheaper metals to cut costs. But notice leadership complacency is to blame in each case.

Today's passage shows us spiritual complacency in Christian leaders can be catastrophic too. When leaders lose sight of God, instead just 'keeping up appearances' or, worse still, using people and ministries for their own ends, then tragically it's often the people of God who suffer most.

Lent is an opportunity for us all to examine our hearts, whether or not we have leadership responsibilities. Hearts that have grown hard in sin are hearts that will be cold towards God.

Take some time to pray for your church leaders. Of course, no leader is perfect. We should resist putting them on unrealistic pedestals. But we should also have high standards for those collectively entrusted with guarding the gospel, pastoring the flock, and contending for the faith.

How does today's passage act as a sombre warning for you and your church context?

_____

 Listen to 'Rise Up' by Bifrost Arts.

The Chase and the Catch

Read Lamentations 4:17–20

UNDER SIEGE

The 2016 movie *The Siege of Jadotville* retells the true story of a contingent of 155 Irish soldiers who are stationed in the Congo as part of a UN peace-keeping mission in 1961. With civil war raging, a 5000-strong mercenary force launches an attack on the isolated Irish, who are positioned in a simple compound with limited weaponry and supplies. The film captures the inevitable terror of siege warfare as an overpowering enemy tightens its grip on those who have nowhere to turn.

We feel that tightening grip in today's reading as the reality of the Babylonians' Jerusalem siege is further unpacked. And just like in chapter 2, we see a transition halfway through the chapter as the harrowing narrative moves from a slightly passive, third-person account to an emotive, first-person perspective. The city itself once again cries for our attention.

WHEN OUR LIFE BREATH FAILS

We saw yesterday how God's people suffered from a colossal failure of leadership (4:13–14). The fail-safe provision of prophets, priests and kings had spectacularly failed! Previously, God had used one of these offices to correct the others: prophets had challenged kings (2 Samuel 12), and kings had exposed the sins of priests (2 Kings 12). But here, devastatingly, this 'triple lock' had let them down; even the king on David's throne, 'the LORD's anointed' (Lamentations 4:20), couldn't help them.

We can imagine the desperate sentries scanning the horizon for any sign that foreign help might be on its way – but there is no cavalry coming (4:17). And even this remark in itself is telling: Judah had a history of making alliances with other nations rather than depending upon God. Now, when it mattered, this strategy of disobedience was shown to be worthless.

CAUGHT IN THE SNARE

Our poet's focus shifts to the anointed king himself, 'our very life breath' (4:20). There had been a steady decline amongst Judah's kings in recent years. When King Jehoiachin was deported after a previous Babylonian attack, his twenty-one-year-old uncle Mattaniah had been installed by the invaders as a puppet king. The Babylonians even renamed him Zedekiah to show their power over the city (see 2 Kings 24:8–17).

However, as 2 Kings 24–25 recounts, Zedekiah also did 'evil in the eyes of the LORD' (24:19). He even managed to wind up the Babylonian king, Nebuchadnezzar, by drawing up alliances with rival nations (24:20). So when the Babylonians encamped around Jerusalem and laid siege, it was clear he was on borrowed time. Consequently, Zedekiah jumped ship, fleeing at night, only to be quickly caught, blinded and sent to Babylon.

To think of the king, God's 'anointed', caught like a frightened animal in a trap is a far cry from the unshakable reign famously promised in Psalm 2. Zedekiah was a king who couldn't even save himself, never mind offering a protective 'shadow' of blessing and security to his people (Lamentations 4:20).

Tragically, God's people had become accustomed to finding refuge in the 'shadow' of unfaithful kings and other gods, but only the Lord can provide such shelter. Psalm 91:1 is sometimes called the Christian's '911'. (British readers: this is the American phone number for emergency services – the equivalent of '999'!) It says, 'Whoever dwells in the shelter of the Most High will rest in the shadow of the Almighty.' Rejoice that we live in Jesus Christ's protective shadow – the shelter of the cross; he is our 'life breath', who breathed his last breath for us. Pray that we'll bask in the sunshine of his gospel until he returns.

 Listen to *'Fell Like a Feather'* by Amy Stroup.

Day 30

The Closest of Enemies

Read Lamentations 4:21–22

PERSECUTION LEADS TO LAMENT

The Christian charity Open Doors reports that over 360 million Christians suffer persecution and discrimination worldwide. From Somalia to Syria and the Maldives to Myanmar, believers are sidelined, mistreated and even killed for following Jesus Christ.

Maybe you're facing a situation with some measure of injustice or pressure because of your Christian faith? Today's passage helps us lament in the face of such abuse – and as it brings us to the end of this penultimate chapter of Lamentations, it also lifts our eyes to the future.

BE CAREFUL WHO YOU SCORN

The poet addresses two specific groups of people: 'Daughter Edom' and 'Daughter Zion'. To understand these names, we need to press 'rewind' and trace the history of God's people back to Genesis. One of the patriarchs, Jacob (renamed by God as 'Israel', and the son of Isaac and grandson of Abraham), also had an older brother, Esau, from whom the nation of Edom was descended.

A sibling rivalry ensued between Jacob and Esau, bitterly played out in Genesis 25–33 and later replicated in the tensions between Israel and Edom (see, for example, Numbers 20:14; Deuteronomy 2:4–5; Amos 1:11). This all came to a bitter head as the Edomites cheered on the Babylonian army when they ravaged Israel's historic capital, Jerusalem (Psalm 137:7). But, as the prophet Obadiah makes very clear, this contempt would not be forgotten by God (Obadiah 10–15).

YOUR TIME WILL COME

Throughout the Bible, facing God's righteous anger is described as drinking a 'cup'. The poet tells us this cup will soon be passed to Edom (Lamentations 4:21). Like an intoxicating wine that terrifyingly overpowers all who must drink it to the dregs, this righteous judgment will be unbearable. Effectively the message is, 'Enjoy laughing whilst you can, Edom, because you too will face God's judgment soon enough' (4:21).

And with this marked declaration of judgment upon Jerusalem's enemies, there is suddenly now hope for God's people. Referring to them tenderly as 'Daughter Zion', the poet declares that their punishment and exile *will* have an expiry date. There is an 'end' in sight (4:22).

LEARNING TO CRY, 'HOW LONG?'

Historians think Edom was conquered just a few decades after the Babylonian invasion of Jerusalem, then gradually disappeared as an entity over the subsequent centuries. But whilst Edom has faced its punishment, Christians are still longing for Jesus to vindicate his persecuted people by overthrowing their enemies.

But maybe we've lost sight of our persecuted brothers and sisters around the world? Maybe we don't lament their suffering because they're just not on our spiritual radar? And if that's the case, maybe that means we've also settled for a consumeristic approach to religion – maybe it means our focus is ourselves and our comfort here and now?

The apostle John is given a vision of those Christians who have been killed for their faith:

'They called out in a loud voice, 'How long, Sovereign Lord, holy and true, until you judge the inhabitants of the earth and avenge our blood?' Then each of them was given a white robe, and they were told to wait a little longer…' (Revelation 6:10–11).

Are you holding onto that promise of a 'little while longer', or are you living like you're already at home? Are you joining in their cry, 'How long…?' or are you unmoved by the mistreatment of Christians, locally or globally?

 Listen to *'The Reckoning (How Long)'* by Andrew Peterson.

Day 31

Life in the Shadowlands

Read Romans 1:18–32

EVERY DAY IS A MINI JUDGMENT DAY

Most of us probably think about 'judgment day' as a *future* event. But as we feel the devastating social impact of God's wrath upon Jerusalem in Lamentations 4, it's a reminder that God's judgment is something our world experiences in the *present* too. As the apostle Paul says, 'The wrath of God *is being revealed* from heaven against all the godlessness and wickedness of people' (Romans 1:18; my italics).

To understand this, we need to follow the apostle's logic. God's creation tells us enough about our Creator that every single one of us should turn to him in worship and wonder (1:19–20). Yet tragically none of us honour God as we ought. Paul illustrates this with three instances of humanity 'exchanging' the worship of God for patterns of living that do not glorify him (1:23, 25, 26). In response to these three examples, we have three 'matching' instances of God giving us over to what we desire (1:24, 26, 28). In other words, humanity actively substitutes God for other things, and in response God actively expresses his wrath by, surprisingly, giving us what we ask for.

TURKEYS VOTING FOR CHRISTMAS

Think of it like this: we 'vote' for a life without God calling the shots, and God's judgment is that this is what we get. Yet as the societal chaos of Lamentations 4 shows, a life without God is truly horrifying. Value, dignity and divinely bestowed honour are gradually lost from our society and culture; we become less human. This is also captured in Romans 1, where our bodies, desires and minds bear the consequences of turning away from God's purposes for us (1:24, 26, 28).

What we thought was a vote for our 'freedom' was in reality opting for a dehumanising life sentence. It's like turkeys blindly voting for Christmas – or Thanksgiving, if you're American!

SHADOWS OF A GREATER JUDGMENT

Why would God do this? Theologian Dan Strange frames this present experience of God's wrath as like living among the 'shadows' of God's final judgment.[21] Yes, there is a final judgment day to come, which will reveal fully both how great the offence of our rebellion is and how terrible a life is without any of God's good gifts and gracious presence. But that final judgment casts its shadows upon life now. In the present consequences of every sinful act and thought, we get a taste of the offence of our sin and the horror of a life without God.

And yet even in this wrath, God is also showing mercy. When we step into a shadow, we know we are not in the light. In God's kindness and patience, it can wake us up to repentance (Romans 2:4). As C.S. Lewis famously put it, the experience of suffering can be God's 'megaphone to rouse a deaf world'.[22] Like the prodigal son who asks for and is given his inheritance by his Father, despite the request being an offensive act of treachery, it is often only in the pig pen that we 'come to ourselves' (Luke 15:11–32).

All around us we see attitudes, behaviours and social norms marked by a rejection of God and his word. Do you realise these not only indicate sinful choices, but are also evidence in themselves of God's wrath?

Maybe there are particular aspects of our society or your community that weigh especially on your heart today. Cry out to the Lord for his mercy in saving and renewing our land. And how could you help your friends, family and neighbours see we live in the 'shadowlands'?

 Listen to 'O God of Mercy, Hear Our Plea' by Sovereign Grace Music.

Day 32

Unravelling Words, Unravelling World

Read Lamentations 5:1

THE DISORDER OF SUFFERING

How have you found Lamentations so far? Today, we enter the fifth and final chapter of this heartrending book. There have been high points along the way, but if our poet is taking us on a journey, then this closing chapter is our final resting place.

And even as we begin, there is a vital change which those of us reading in English (rather than the original Hebrew!) could otherwise miss: this is the only chapter *not* written as an acrostic poem – it has *no* clear 'A, B, C...' pattern in the opening letters of each verse. In other words, suddenly the pattern of the other four chapters is disrupted, like someone slamming on the brakes for an emergency stop. Yes, the words continue to flow, but in Hebrew they now come across as rough and disordered. Hebrew readers would be unsettled and taken aback. Why the change?

Someone once said poetry has a knack of letting the truth sneak up on you. It *shows* rather than tells. Here the very *form* of chapter 5 is part of the showing. These disordered words are trying to reflect the reality of suffering itself. Chaotic, disjointed, uncomfortable: we simply can't escape it. This is how life felt in Jerusalem in 586 BC. This is life in a broken, fallen world.

SUFFERING'S BEST RESULT?

Just as with every other chapter, there is again a change of focus. Having moved from 'she' (chapter 1: the city of Jerusalem), to 'he' (chapter 2: God), to 'I' (chapter 3: the man of suffering), to 'they' (chapter 4: the people of the city), chapter 5 focuses on 'we'. It is a collective voice – and we soon notice it is nothing less than a prayer directed to the Lord (5:1).

Our writer is clearly exhausted. He has shared not just third-person observations, but the depths of woe flowing from his own heart as one of God's people. But though he has little left, he shows us that we can *still* pray.

Maybe you've found this season of Lent overwhelming? Maybe it's been emotionally exhausting to face up to your own sin, mortality and brokenness? The pastor and writer Eugene Peterson has said that 'prayer is suffering's best result'.[23] The definition of a Lent well spent is surely to lean on a great Christ.

As we'll discover over the next few days, this book doesn't finish with a tidy resolution. But in the midst of an unravelling world, we can still pray. In fact, God himself has given us these words to pray. Words for sinners. Words of repentance. Words for life.

REMEMBER, REMEMBER

And what about the content of this prayer? Chris Wright has noted that it begins with 'Exodus words' – we're taken back to when the people of Israel were enslaved in Egypt and desperate for God to act in line with his promises. As Wright comments, 'When God remembers, it is not because God has forgotten.'[24] He isn't blind to his people's situation or distracted elsewhere. By asking God to 'remember', we're longing for him to act according to his character and his covenant.

Is your prayer life polished or plain-spoken? Is it refined or real? Do you know it's ok to pray desperate words in a disordered world, as we throw ourselves upon our God and his promises? This chapter will continue to help us do that. Why not echo verse 1 in your own words now...

 Listen to *'Remember'* by Lauren Daigle.

Day 33

As the Dust Settles

Read Lamentations 5:2–8

THE NEW NORMAL

As we all adjusted to the various stages of pandemic life after the Covid-19 outbreak in 2020, one of the buzz phrases was 'the new normal'. It captured that sense of life being different now. Things wouldn't be the same.

And as our poet invites his readers to pray with him to God, he also invites us to face up to 'the new normal' of life in Jerusalem. Though chapter 5 has the familiar twenty-two verse format of the other three outer chapters, here each verse is much shorter and punchier.

Nothing of the content is particularly new to Lamentations, but the blunter feel gives us a grim snapshot of this 'new normal' for God's people. The dust has begun to settle, but things have not got any better. Daily routines have changed and are now unavoidable reminders that this people sinned and faced God's wrath (5:4, 8). In fact, the 'freshness' of Judah's initial suffering seems to have given way to the sapping feeling of its familiarity.

LOST LIFE IN A WORLD UNDER JUDGMENT

We see here a desperate tale of lost homes, lost families, lost essentials and lost freedom. There is an absence of what most of us take for granted. In a bitter irony, a people that were to be marked by their care of orphans and widows are now widows and orphans themselves (5:3).

And yet throughout this inventory of loss, there is no assumption of innocence (5:7, though we'll see this more collectively owned in 5:16). Nor is there any complaint about this treatment. Instead, the prayer models a godly grief at sin. This is lament, as we turn in our sorrow to trust in God afresh, longing for what has been lost.

THE LOSS OF LAMENT

Our situation today is not the same as Jerusalem in 587 BC, but we do live in a world ravaged by sin. When was the last time we found ourselves weeping at the state of the world? When was the last time we cried out to God for mercy for our world?

Mark Vroegop has written about the Western church's discomfort with lament:

> [I]t has been my experience that many Christians are uncomfortable with the tension of the long rehearsing of pain combined with the appeal to God's grace. We tend to hush the recitation of sorrow … I wonder what would happen if more Christians confidently walked into the darkest moments of life and guided people in talking to God about their pain.[25]

Once again, though we cannot directly link all suffering to *particular* instances of sin, we can say that all suffering in the world is a general consequence of humanity's rebellion against God. As such, none of us can avoid suffering. Things aren't as they should be, and lament is about acknowledging that. But rather than responding with directionless moaning, this chapter shows us the importance of a contrite groaning to God as we mourn and grieve the sin that devastates our lives.

Do you tend to respond to suffering in this world with a directionless moaning, or a Godward groaning? How might Lamentations help you respond to your own sin and the 'everyday' sin in the world around us? Rejoice that though this is our 'normal', one day it will cease and we will enjoy a 'new normal' beyond our greatest hopes and wildest dreams.

 Listen to *'Land of the Living (Psalm 27:13)'* by Carolyn Arends.

Day 34

Shame on You

Read Lamentations 5:9–16

WALK OF SHAME

Today, we enter Holy Week, the final week of this Lent season. As I've reflected on Lamentations 5, it's helped me to see how much the hours and days before Jesus' death were so full of *shame*.

Shame is a funny word, and notoriously difficult to define. For a start, it's invisible! And yet most of us would probably be able to identify its impact upon someone – or upon ourselves. We know shame when we feel it.

But think about Jesus' last moments: having proclaimed himself to be God's Messiah, he was then betrayed with a kiss, abandoned by his friends and handed over to foreign authorities. He was put before a sham trial, complete with false witnesses, only to be sentenced to crucifixion in place of a renowned murderer. He was stripped, flogged and mocked, with a crown of thorns placed upon his head. Then finally, after being made to carry his own cross, he was hung up upon it. And any last remaining scrap of dignity would have been snatched away in crucifixion itself, as the cruel torture forced Jesus to gradually and very publicly lose all control of his body and mind. His vital organs would have shut down one by one as he slowly died one of the most agonising and humiliating deaths ever devised by humanity.

Shame? It doesn't even come close.

SEEING DISGRACE

How does this relate to Lamentations? In this final chapter, we're tracing the closing and collective lament of God's people. The poet began by calling upon the Lord to 'remember' them (5:1), but he didn't stop there. He pleaded with God to 'look, and see our disgrace' (5:1). That final word reveals a deep sense of shame.

And in today's verses, we see this shame played out: God's people are risking their lives just to hunt for scraps of food (5:9). Their women are exposed to abuse and assault in their own homeland (5:11). Authority figures are mocked and brutally shown to be powerless (5:12). Their disobedience has led to their shaming.

REDEEMING SHAME?

Many today describe shame as a destructive feeling. The author and speaker Brené Brown famously appeared on Oprah Winfrey's TV show to declare that shame is 'lethal'. But should we be so determined to rid our world of *all* forms of shame?

Throughout Lamentations, our poet has been unflinchingly blunt that the behaviour of God's people warranted their punishment. They had not only disobeyed God, but had dishonoured him. But by the end of today's reading, they make a remarkable confession: 'Woe to us, for we have sinned!' (5:16).

Christian professor Te-Li Lau makes the following claim: 'as a human emotion, shame is a necessary element of who we are; as a moral emotion, shame is a critical component of our moral apparatus.'[26] Rather than denying their shame, rather than passing the blame, the people of Jerusalem *own* the shame of their sin. After all, this was not about having broken some arbitrary rules. And so the poet gives words to help us acknowledge the gravity of dishonouring the God who has set his steadfast love upon us.

The seventeenth-century Christian pastor Thomas Watson helpfully talked about a 'holy bashfulness'. Just like the poet in Lamentations, our shame-filled sin should drive us to run to God in faith-filled lament, rather than to flee from him. For he is a God who was shamed for the sake of the shameful. He experienced a disgrace like no other, so that he can restore the disgraced.

 Listen to *'From the Depths of Woe (Psalm 130)'* by Indelible Grace Music, featuring Andrew Osenga and Emily Deloach.

Clinging to the Throne

Read Lamentations 5:17–19

THE BODY KEEPS SCORE

'The Body Keeps the Score' has become a common phrase in recent years.[27] It captures the reality that suffering and trauma often leave their mark within our bodies. And as our poet continues to lead his people in collective lament, we see that truth here too: 'our hearts are faint' and 'our eyes grow dim' (5:17). This is no surprise in light of all that they have experienced, understood and confessed, but perhaps we can sometimes underestimate how much our spiritual health can impact our physical health? If the body keeps the score, the poet's body is declaring a devastating one-sided defeat.

And perhaps the losses of the last sixteen verses are now epitomised in 5:18: 'Mount Zion ... lies desolate' with wild animals 'prowling' over its ruins. It's the only time in Lamentations that the poet refers to Jerusalem with this moniker, but the resplendent title captures the rich history and geographical strength of the city (see, for example, Psalm 48:1–3). Yet now it is a wasteland.

Facing that predicament, what would you cling on to?

THE THRONE IS NOT EMPTY

As we'll see in the final verses tomorrow, Lamentations is not a book where all the loose ends are tied up neatly. In this present life, there is much that will remain unresolved. But whilst the sheer weight of our questions and emotions deserves more than simplistic answers, there is a simple acknowledgment that rings out: 'You, LORD, reign for ever; your throne endures from generation to generation' (5:19). Simple yes, but not simplistic.

What's prompted this? Notice that the poet *hasn't* suddenly been told breaking news of some victorious event. His circumstances haven't changed at all. And yet in the middle of this desolation, the poet reorientates his heart to one truth: God's sovereignty over everything, including our pain. God is not distant. His throne is not empty. Though the physical kingdom is in ruins, a spiritual kingdom endures through those ruins. This present suffering is not the end of the story.

SOVEREIGNTY AND SUFFERING

To say these words in the midst of cancer or miscarriage or chronic pain or financial stress might seem crazy: *Doesn't this suffering show you there can't be a good God?! How can you still believe when this is happening?*

Suffering often cuts through abstract theology and takes us to the heart of matters. But Lamentations 5 is not abstract theology. We know that our poet is not detached from the reality of life. He's wandered around the ruins of his decimated city and seen things we'd never wish to see. We mustn't now patronise him by telling him he doesn't know about suffering.

Lamentations has been full of grief, tears and questions. There have been doubts, wrestling and rage. I hope this book has helped you understand such responses aren't 'wrong' and can be brought *to* God. But there is a sure ground upon which our protest, struggle and confusion can rest: God is God and he reigns forever.

Amidst the messy realities of life, how might you be able to share 5:19 as a prayer? Wonderfully, as Christians, we know that our king took off his crown and stepped into this fallen, broken world to restore it. Now Jesus reigns as the crucified, risen and ascended Lord. His throne is not empty – and one day we'll see him reigning on it.

 Listen to *'You're Still God'* by Philippa Hanna.

When the Ends Remain Untied

Read Lamentations 5:20–22

MESSY ENDINGS

When it comes to suffering, Lamentations, refreshingly, helps to both set our expectations and guide our response. Yesterday, our poet affirmed God's sovereign rule. But with those words still hanging in the air, he now brings his book of lament to its actual close – with a question, a plea and a lingering doubt.

WHY?

First come the questions: 'Why… Why…?' (5:20). That's the perennial question, the ache of every suffering human heart. We read it on notes attached to flowers following a tragedy. We hear it mouthed from grieving lips. Sometimes it's uttered in inconsolable sadness; other times it's shouted in utter rage. This is the lived experience of feeling forgotten and forsaken.

Lamentations has not been silent in providing 'answers'. There has been confession of sin and acceptance of judgment. As Christians, we theoretically know *why* this world is broken. We also know Jesus is restoring it – and that God is sovereign over it.

Yet the questions and tensions remain. As we've seen, it's crucial these are given space and brought to God. This is what it means to lament. Perhaps some of us might not be accustomed to framing them as sharply as here. But even if we haven't explicitly raged at God or wept until it hurts, we may well have silently struggled to make sense of our experiences, or been living with a lingering sense of being forgotten. As Alianore Smith puts it, 'Simply naming your suffering before God ... is a powerful act of faith, even if at the time it just feels like complaining.'[28]

RETURN...

Despite the NIV translation, the same word, often translated as 'return' or 'turn back', occurs twice in 5:21: 'Cause us to [re]turn, Lord, to you, and we shall [re]turn.'[29] This is fascinating and pastorally apt; they do not plead with God to come to them in deliverance.

The shock is that the book's closing plea is not for the enemy to be driven away, or Jerusalem to be rebuilt, or even for all the suffering to end. The poet knows what God's people need most of all is God himself. And who can provide that need but God? The initiative flows from him, entirely in keeping with God's promises of changing their hearts to love him (Deuteronomy 30:6).

UNLESS?

Finally, what about 5:22 for a cliffhanger! In fact, the sense of unresolved tension has meant many Jewish synagogues rearrange the closing verses, reading 5:21 *after* 5:22! But Bible teacher Di Warren perceptively observes that many Western Christians do our own rearranging, replacing 5:22 with 3:22. In other words, we want to focus on God's unfailing compassion, not his anger 'beyond measure'.[30] And yet the final attribute of God mentioned by our poet is God's wrath, as he wonders what future awaits God's people.

But even here our poet doubts not God's character but his own relationship with God. He is experiencing life in a world under God's judgment, and so can hardly comprehend God's great love. His instinct is self-doubt rather than entitlement or assumption.

I hope it encourages you that Lamentations doesn't end with all the loose ends tied up because, after all, that's not what most of life is like! Maybe you're living in the middle of such unresolved tension at the moment? We know the truth of God's gospel promise – of Jesus dying and rising for us – but the lived reality often feels different. How do these words give voice to the lament of your heart?

 Listen to *'Hard to Get – demo version'* by Rich Mullins.

Day 37

The Look

Read Lamentations 1:1–4 and Luke 22:7–38, 54–62

A THURSDAY LIKE NO OTHER

As we enter the final days of what is often called Holy Week, we're going to revisit some particular passages from Lamentations and read them alongside the Gospels.

The day before he is crucified, Jesus gathers with his disciples for a Passover meal, as was the Jewish custom. But as Jesus breaks bread and shares wine, he reinterprets the meal as being about his body and blood – 'a new covenant' (Luke 22:20). Stunningly (and to some protest) he also washes his disciples' feet in an act of humble service (John 13:1–17). In doing so, he gives his disciples a trailer of his servant-hearted and sin-cleansing death. The name often given for today, Maundy Thursday, comes from the Latin word mandatum, meaning 'commandment'. This is because it is here that Jesus gives his disciples a 'new command', to 'love one another [as] I have loved you' (John 13:34).

ONE LOOK

Today is clearly a day filled with rich imagery and tangible moments; there's so much that we could focus on. But this Maundy Thursday, I want us to cast our eyes on a brief exchange between Jesus and the apostle Peter. It comes after Simon Peter has pledged to be with Jesus 'to death' (Luke 22:33), only to be told by his Lord that he will deny Jesus three times before 'the rooster crows' (22:34).

Most of us will know what happens next: Jesus is betrayed by his disciple Judas, seized by officers of the temple guard, taken away and temporarily imprisoned at the house of the high priest. When Peter follows at a distance, sure enough, three times he is recognised as a disciple of Jesus, only to deny him each time (22:54–60). And then the rooster crows. But have you ever spotted this line in Luke's account: 'The Lord turned and looked straight at Peter' (22:61)?

Grasping that Jesus was within eyesight of Peter brings a whole extra layer of betrayal, guilt and shame to this moment. What was that 'look' like? Luke can only tell us what response it brought about in Peter: the apostle 'remembered the word the Lord had spoken to him … he went outside and wept bitterly' (22:61–62).

HEART-PIERCING AND HEART-HEALING

There is nothing hidden from Jesus' gaze. This is how the nineteenth-century English pastor Charles Spurgeon imagines Jesus' look:

> I think it was a heart-piercing look and a heart-healing look all in one,— a look which revealed to Peter the blackness of his sin, and also the tenderness of his Master's heart towards him.[31]

Though our tears may be bitter, this is the One who has stooped from his heavenly throne to wash us clean of our sin. This is the One who provided his own body and blood to feed our hearts with that which truly satisfies our spiritual hunger. This is the One who walked towards those who betray him, knowing those steps would make forgiveness possible for his betrayers.

Throughout Lent we will no doubt have felt the burden of our failure, brokenness and sin. Like Jerusalem in Lamentations, maybe we have felt it hanging like a slave's yoke on our necks (1:14). Fearful or ashamed, perhaps at times we have felt unable to turn our gaze to God. But if we lift our heads in faith and repentance, if we look Jesus in the eye, then we too will see his heart-piercing and heart-healing look.

 Listen to *'Steadfast Love'* by Shane & Shane.

Day 38

Lamenting on Good Friday

Read Lamentations 2:8–10; 3:19–21 and Matthew 27:32–56

SORROWFUL FRIDAY?

Of all the days to lament, surely today, when we especially remember Jesus' death, is particularly worthy of our sorrow? For that reason, the name 'Good Friday' can often cause confusion or feel grating. This is especially so in a culture that's increasingly biblically illiterate; I've lost count of how often I've been asked why Christians call a gruesome death 'good'? Maybe we should follow the Germans, who call today *Karfreitag* or 'Sorrowful Friday'…

But for those who *have* grasped the significance of Jesus' death, we see this day's stunning goodness amidst the sorrow.

A DREADFUL DAY

Historically, some Christians have read the above passages from Lamentations on Good Friday. They certainly take on fresh significance alongside Matthew's account of the crucifixion.

Our slow journey through Lamentations has given us various camera angles on the destruction of Jerusalem in 587 BC. It was a devastating spectacle, but the unanimous testimony of Lamentations is that it was the Lord's work (2:8). The only response to such a traumatic and humiliating experience could be silence, grief and shock (2:10).

Reading Matthew's Gospel, we see that the crucifixion of Jesus was another 'dreadful' work of God. There was the sudden midday darkness, with its deep biblical associations of the judgment of God

(Matthew 27:45). Then there was the apparent God-forsakenness of the man on the cross (27:46). And there was the bleak and blatant hopelessness of death, visible to all looking on (27:50). So whilst Matthew doesn't describe the watching women's reaction (27:55–56), it's not unreasonable to imagine them weeping with heads bowed to the ground.

Likewise, as we read of Jesus being offered gall to drink (27:34), we think of the testimony of the sufferer in Lamentations 3:19. 'Gall' often referred to a bitter wine, typically offered to criminals before their execution as a small mercy to reduce their suffering. But after tasting the gall, Jesus refuses it, presumably so that he could face the cross with a clear mind. John records that later, in Jesus' final moments, a sponge was soaked in wine vinegar and lifted on a hyssop stalk to his lips (John 19:29–30).

PREPARING FOR THE CROSS

In many ways, the horror of Lamentations prepares us for Good Friday by showing that sin is serious and God's judgment cannot be ignored. Yet the wonder of comparing these two dreadful days is that there is a striking difference: on Good Friday the Man of Sorrows came to pay a debt he did not owe, because we owed a debt we could not pay. So yes, we lament the weight of our own selfishness, lovelessness and pride, but we also rejoice that they have been dealt with. We make our way to the cross of Christ 'trembling yet hopeful'.[32]

Only a few days ago, we considered the closing words of Lamentations: 'Restore us to yourself, Lord, that we may return' (5:21). The stunning shock of Scripture is that *this* day, Good Friday, is where we see what it took for God to answer that prayer. The cross of Jesus Christ is God's costly response. As the apostle Paul puts it, for our sake 'God made [Christ] who had no sin to be sin for us, so that in him we might become the righteousness of God' (2 Corinthians 5:21).

As we gaze at the cross of Christ today, let us bow our heads in the silence, turn from our sin afresh and come to Jesus in faith. Why not express your trust in his saving death through the simple closing prayer of Lamentations 5:21.

 Listen to *'Look Again'* by 20schemes Music.

The Dark Before the Dawn

Read Lamentations 3:37–58 and Matthew 27:62–66

SILENCE'S WITNESS

With Saturday being the Jewish Sabbath, there is a pause in activity, but the chief priests and Pharisees are concerned that Jesus' body might be stolen. Consequently, Pilate seals the tomb with a stone and scales up the Roman guard (Matthew 27:62–66). Yet from Jesus himself, or even those who followed him, there seems to be only *silence*.

In fact, silence is a word that captures today, Holy Saturday, well. We read elsewhere that the disciples had been hiding in fear (John 20:19). In the preceding hours, their leader had been arrested, tried and then brutally crucified. The record had stopped playing. The lines had gone dead. How might you have responded to that silence?

LIFE IN THE DARK

As we come back today to these verses from Lamentations 3, they give us a prophetic glimpse of the events of Jerusalem in 33 AD. The Saviour of the world lay in a deathly pit (3:53). The full weight of the curse of sin had been borne in our place (3:43). This lonely man had cried out from the cross in piercing agony to his God and Father (3:55). We can imagine his desperate pleas echoing eerily around that darkened Jerusalem hillside before silence descended. Swallowed up by death, Jesus committed himself into his Father's hands and breathed his last – for now (3:54).

Over the centuries, some Christians have marked today with a special service called *Tenebrae* – a Latin word meaning 'darkness' or 'shadows'. Lit candles are slowly snuffed out, one by one, until the room is in total darkness. It's a dramatic depiction that tells two stories. Firstly, the abandonment Christ faced from his disciples before his death. One by one they scattered, leaving him alone, bar the women who watched from a distance (Matthew 27:55–56). But secondly, it portrays Jesus' own loss of life. The light of the world was 'snuffed out' and now lay dead in a grave. Creation itself had been plunged into silent darkness.

SILENCE DOES NOT MEAN ABSENCE

Christians can rush past this day too quickly. We've rejoiced in the mercy of the cross shown on Good Friday, and now we're eager to join in the celebrations of Easter Sunday. But today we're invited to pause in the silence.

Have you ever had a season of life where you wake up in the small hours because heavy matters are weighing on your mind? And then you wait endlessly for the dawn? This is Holy Saturday. Someone said it's like the space between a full stop at the end of one sentence and the capital letter that begins the next.

Actually, life is *full* of moments like this. Waiting. Disappointment. Silence. Yet even the utter hopelessness of death is a place Jesus has been. He is no stranger to the darkest valley you could ever walk.

So whilst tomorrow will be a day for celebrating God's redeeming goodness (cf. Lamentations 3:58), today helps us see our faith can bear the weight of this silence. Christianity is not about a trite positivity that is tone-deaf to our unanswered questions and unfulfilled hopes. Saturday's silence does not mean a Saviour's absence.

Creator of heaven and earth, we ask that, just as the crucified body of your dear Son was laid in the tomb and rested on this Holy Saturday, help us to await with him the coming of our 'third day' when we shall rise with him to newness of life. And in the silence of that waiting, may we still be aware of your presence. Amen. (Adapted from the Book of Common Prayer)

 Listen to *'The Dark Before the Dawn'* by Andrew Peterson.

Hope in the Valley of Tears

Read John 20:1–18

WHY ARE YOU CRYING?

Happy Easter! Today, Christians take time to celebrate that, two thousand years ago, Jesus conquered death. But on this day of rejoicing, have you ever noticed how the risen Jesus' first words are about *tears*: 'Woman, why are you crying?' (John 20:15).

At first glance it seems an odd question. After all, leaving debates about Jesus' divine foreknowledge to one side, surely Jesus could have guessed why Mary Magdalene was overcome with grief?! Didn't he understand how human relationships worked?

But as we dwell upon those words, I hope you see a precious truth for us today: the risen Jesus sees our tears. The NLT translation better captures Jesus' tenderness here: 'Dear woman...' It's as if he envelopes this grieving woman with love, assuring her that her deep sorrow is seen.

Initially, Mary doesn't even recognise Jesus. So as he addresses her, he seems to focus on the person behind the grief: 'Woman, why are you crying? Who is it you are looking for?' (John 20:15). Finally, he calls her name, 'Mary'; only then does she realise just who he is (20:16).

LIFE IN THE VALE OF TEARS

Jesus was no stranger to tears. Earlier in John's Gospel, we read how Jesus wept in anguish at the tomb of his friend Lazarus (11:35). As he later approached his own death, Jesus told his followers that they would 'weep and mourn' (16:20).

In other words, Jesus knew well that life is full of tears. Sometimes this world is even described as 'the vale of tears', an enduring phrase originating from old translations of Psalm 84:6. It resonates so much with life as we know it.

Lamentations has also been a valley of tears in so many ways. Its pages have been soaked with weeping, and drenched with the uncomfortable ache of sin, suffering and sorrow. Maybe part of you will be glad to step out of its dark depths?

OPERATION NO MORE TEARS

When Jesus asks Mary about her tears, he's not accusing her of some inappropriate response. Far from it. We might say he is showing the connection between her tears and his identity as her risen Saviour.

In her bestselling children's devotional, *The Jesus Storybook Bible*, author Sally Lloyd-Jones describes God's cosmic purpose as 'Operation No More Tears'. It's a beautiful way of capturing the goal of Jesus' cross-shaped mission.

As Mary and Jesus knew all too well, the day of 'no more tears' has not yet arrived. This is an age of lament. But though we continue to weep through the 'night', we know 'rejoicing comes in the morning' (Psalm 30:5). Today, as we recall Jesus stepping out of that grave, having tackled sin and death head on, we can be sure that joyful morning will one day dawn. He sees our tears now, and one day he will personally wipe each tear from our eyes (Revelation 21:4).

Well, it's been quite an intense forty days! But I hope you've seen how Lamentations' piercing, emotional grasp of reality is much needed for the Christian life. Perhaps you've never really known that it's ok for Christians to be honest about sorrow and hardship? Maybe you've come away eager to build rhythms of lament into your life or the life of your church?

Why not find some time in the coming days to process with God what he's laid on your heart from his word. What do you want to maintain from this journey of lament? But, for now, rejoice that Jesus is risen and he sees your tears; and that changes everything.

'Be still, my soul: the hour is hast'ning on
When we shall be forever with the Lord.
When disappointment, grief, and fear are gone,
Sorrow forgot, love's purest joys restored.
Be still, my soul: when change and tears are past
All safe and blessed we shall meet at last.'

(Katerina von Schlegel, 'Be Still My Soul')

 Listen to 'Eternal Weight of Glory' by Wendell Kimbrough.

Notes

1 Leslie C. Allen, *Liturgy of Grief: A Pastoral Commentary on Lamentations* (Baker Academic, 2011).

2 Mark Vroegop, '5 Reasons You Should Preach Through Lamentations' (9Marks, 11 September 2018): https://www.9marks.org/article/lamentations/

3 Charles Wesley (1707–88), 'All ye that pass by, to Jesus draw nigh'.

4 Keith Kahn-Harris, 'Denialism: What Drives People to Reject the Truth' (*The Guardian*, 3 August 2018): https://www.theguardian.com/news/2018/aug/03/denialism-what-drives-people-to-reject-the-truth

5 John Donne (1572–1631), 'The Lamentations of Jeremy, for the most part according to Tremelius' in *Chapters into Verse: Poetry in English Inspired by the Bible*, eds Robert Atwan and Laurance Wieder, vol. 1 (Oxford University Press, 1993), pp. 418–20.

6 G.K. Chesterton, *Orthodoxy* (first published 1908), p. 10.

7 Dietrich Bonhoeffer, *The Cost of Discipleship* (first published by Macmillan, 1949).

8   I owe this illustration to writer Matthew Becklo on his blog 'Word on Fire': https://www.wordonfire.org/articles/in-defense-of-bitter-lamentations/

9   Alianore Smith: https://licc.org.uk/resources/lamentations-2

10   Mark Vroegop, *Dark Clouds, Deep Mercy: Discovering the Grace of Lament* (Crossway, 2019), p. 10.

11   Miroslav Volf, *Free of Charge* (Zondervan, 2009), pp. 138–39.

12   I owe this imagery to C.J. Williams, *The Shadow of Christ in the Book of Lamentations* (Crown and Covenant, 2022), p. 332.

13   I also owe this phrase to C.J. Williams, *The Shadow of Christ in the Book of Lamentations*, p. 332.

14   Christopher Wright, *The Message of Lamentations* in *The Bible Speaks Today* series (IVP, 2015), p. 108.

15   Barry Webb, *Five Festal Garments* (Apollos, 2000), p. 68.

16   Sally Lloyd-Jones, *The Jesus Storybook Bible* (Zonderkidz, 2007).

17   Barbara Brown Taylor, *Leaving Church: A Memoir of Faith* (Canterbury Press, 2011), pp. 147–48.

18   Amanda Thompson, 'Waiting is important, here's why': https://newspring.cc/articles/waiting-is-important-heres-why5

19   Tim Keller, *Walking with God through Pain and Suffering* (Hodder & Stoughton, 2015), pp. 289–90.

20   Mike Ovey, 'The Grace of God OR the World of the West?': https://www.gafcon.org/resources/the-grace-of-god-or-the-world-of-the-west

21 Dan Strange, in Tim Keller's *Loving the City* (Zondervan, 2016), p. 97.

22 C.S. Lewis, *The Problem of Pain* (first published in 1940; this edition: HarperCollins, 2001), pp. 88–89.

23 Eugene H. Peterson, *Five Smooth Stones for Pastoral Work* (William B Eerdmans Publishing Co, 1996), p. 132.

24 Christopher Wright, *The Message of Lamentations*, p. 150.

25 Mark Vroegop, *Dark Clouds, Deep Mercy*, p. 144.

26 Dr Te-Li Lau, 'Defending Shame': https://honorshame.com/defending-shame

27 The phrase 'The Body Keeps the Score' is the title of Bessel van der Kolk's bestselling book (Viking, 2014).

28 See https://licc.org.uk/resources/lamentations-5/

29 This wording is based on Christopher Wright's translation in *The Message of Lamentations*, pp. 159–60.

30 See https://www.equip.org.au/equip22-library-page

31 C.H. Spurgeon, 'Peter's Fall and Restoration' in *The Metropolitan Tabernacle Pulpit Sermons, vol. 48,* (Passmore & Alabaster, 1902), p. 138.

32 Barry Webb, *Five Festal Garments*, p. 81.

10 Publishing

a division of 10 of those.com

10Publishing is the publishing house of **10ofThose**.
It is committed to producing quality Christian resources
that are biblical and accessible.

www.10ofthose.com is our online retail arm selling
thousands of quality books at discounted prices.

For information contact: **info@10ofthose.com**
or check out our website: **www.10ofthose.com**